THE LITTLE BOOK OF

JACK THE RIPPER

THE WHITECHAPEL SOCIETY

The History Press

First published 2014

The History Press
The Mill, Brimscombe Port
Stroud, Gloucestershire, GL5 2QG
www.thehistorypress.co.uk

British Library Cataloguing in Publication Data.
A catalogue record for this book is available from the British Library.

ISBN 978 0 7509 5839 4

Typesetting and origination by The History Press
Printed in Great Britain

Contents

Introduction

It is now 126 years since the 'Autumn of Terror'. Tom Cullen christened the months of August to November 1888 with this chilling title in his book of the same name, published in 1965.

Indeed the East End of London, if not the whole of London, was gripped with increasing terror as a murderer walked the streets of Spitalfields and Whitechapel and slew at least five women.

There was a spate of letters written to the police, the press and others, all purporting to be from the killer. In one letter the writer gave himself the title 'Jack the Ripper' and henceforth, this unknown person has continued to bear that name.

The Little Book of Jack the Ripper plots the story of the murderer as well as the legacy of those crimes and is written by members and friends of The Whitechapel Society. Each chapter is written by a different person, all of whom are very knowledgeable about the Jack the Ripper crimes and each has a particular interest in their chosen chapter.

This book follows on from the success of The Whitechapel Society's earlier books: *Jack the Ripper: The Suspects* (The History Press, 2011) and *Jack the Ripper: The Terrible Legacy* (The History Press, 2013).

The Society is very grateful to the contributors of this and their previous books, who have given so willingly and freely of their time and efforts. The royalties for all the books have gone to the Society to help in the advancement of the aims and objectives of the club. Frogg Moody worked tirelessly on the illustrations and our thanks must also go to The History Press for the support and guidance we have had from them in our book-writing ventures.

The Whitechapel Society (formerly The Cloak & Dagger Club) was founded in 1995 by Mark Galloway. Mark's first real interest in 'Jack' came about when, as a 12-year-old lad, he came across a book in his local library on the history of the Metropolitan Police, which contained a whole chapter on the Whitechapel Murders and Jack the Ripper. What really interested Mark, like so many of us, was the fact that the killer was never caught. Mark (now lifelong honorary president of The Whitechapel Society) is rightly proud of the success that it is today. The aim of the Society was, and still is, to foster the advancement of studies into the Whitechapel Murders and the social history of the Victorian and Edwardian East End of London. The Society is run by a hard-working committee and there is now a thriving website, as well as bi-monthly meetings at which a guest speaker will give a lecture and a bi-monthly journal which goes out to the Society's members. The Society currently numbers 300, some forty of which are non-UK. The Whitechapel Society Journal has developed from the two sides of A4 newsletter in 1995 to a twenty-six-page magazine in 2014. It regularly attracts many contributors, with articles of every description, from well-known authors to amateurs (and often very good ones) trying their hand for the first time.

In recent years the Society has broadened its horizons even further and has explored new and exciting ways to bring the past to life. Members have been invited to participate in a whole host of events, including a photographic history of London's old East End, short story competitions and events days or weekends. To mark the launch of *Jack the Ripper: The Terrible Legacy* the Society held a 'Legacy Weekend' in August 2013. The Saturday started with a trip to the Bishopsgate Institute, followed by speakers and an exciting session of 'Speed History' at the Crosse Keys in Gracechurch Street. On the Sunday, there was a trip to Dennis Severs' House in Folgate Street followed by a conducted walk around 'the Spitalfields that nobody knows'. More recently, members enjoyed a 'Kray Walk', which was led by the Society's former chair and now vice president, Bill Beadle. These are just a couple of examples of what the Society has been able to offer its members.

In 2011, the Society had its first two-day residential conference at the City Hotel in Osborn Street, right in the heart of 'Ripper Country'. It was a sell-out event, attracting delegates from both home and abroad, with high-quality speakers. The after-dinner speaker on the Saturday evening was none other than this country's national treasure, Roy Hudd. Roy, as well as being a very funny and lovely man, is a renowned expert on old-time musical hall. The Society will be holding another two-day conference, this time in Salisbury, Wiltshire, in November 2014.

So if you are new to the study of Jack the Ripper, or indeed have had a festering interest for some time, you will enjoy this book. Not only because of the factual content, but because you will pick up the passion with which all the authors write. Many of them have included a list of books for further reading and/or bibliographies at the end of their chapters and you will find this an excellent resource for guiding your further studies.

If you would like to become a member of The Whitechapel Society and enjoy the immense benefits of being closely associated with a community of historical experts, enthusiasts and aficionados, please go to our website at www.whitechapelsociety.com.

Susan Parry, September 2014
Treasurer – The Whitechapel Society

1

Mary Ann 'Polly' Nichols: The Terror Begins

Ian Parson

Mary Ann was born in 1845 in Shoe Lane off Fleet Street in the heart of old London Town. She came from an average family, lived in an average street and at the age of 19 married William Nichols, a Fleet Street printer. They settled down to begin their life together. Survival for the working class was very hard in those days; even safe drinking water was many years away so weak beer was preferred by the young and old alike. This led to many developing a taste for alcohol.

By her fifth child in 1879, Mary Ann had more or less given up on family bliss and her all-consuming passion was now gin (or 'mother's ruin' as it was more commonly known). She was not a jolly, social drinker; she was an unpredictable, aggressive and troublesome drunk. Her alcohol-fuelled antics would have been tolerated if she was a man but being female she was an embarrassment to the whole family. In Victorian London, in respectable Fleet Street, it still mattered what your neighbours thought.

In 1880 her husband could take her behaviour no more and evicted her from the family home. This was the way things were done back then; a wife was no more than the property of her husband and William thought the best way to resolve the issue was to get rid of his embarrassing partner. He promised her 5*s* a week and threw her on to the mercy of the parish.

She would never again have a home

Mary Ann moved in and out of a succession of workhouses, broken up with brief stays at her father's in Camberwell, South London. Then, in early 1888, she had a stroke of good luck. The workhouse arranged a respectable job for her. She was to be a live-in serving maid in the teetotal, god-fearing house of Mrs Chowdry and family in Wandsworth.

However, on 12 May 1888, only two months into her new employment, she inexplicably stole some clothing and fled. At this point, whether she knew it or not, she had nearly reached the place that all alcoholics and addicts eventually descend to – rock bottom.

Mary Ann, now a fugitive, changed her name to 'Polly' and settled for the wretched existence of sharing one room in a dosshouse slum with five other women. Her new address was No. 18 Thrawl Street, right in the heart of the notorious, crime-ridden East End badlands that crossed the boundary between Whitechapel and Spitalfields. Living in a flea-infested rat hole, Polly and her friends sold themselves for the price of a drink. Wandsworth, although only a few short miles across the Thames, might as well have been on a different planet for her now.

In Wandsworth she had been discouraged from drinking; religion and conformity were the mainstays of daily life. In Whitechapel, drinking was the religion and nonconformity ran deep.

Polly had made her choice and now she would have to live with it.

A drunk

Nowadays we know that Polly needed help to overcome her illness. In 1888, it was considered that those like her couldn't handle their drink and should help themselves. Suggestions as to what they should actually do were unfortunately very thin on the ground: some thought they should pray more, or save a few pennies back for those rainy days. Others felt God was punishing those that chose to live in such squalor and God had a reason for everything – if he saw fit for such people to exist alongside the extreme wealth in the City, well, very few felt they had the right to question God's motives.

The police, meanwhile, had better things to do then go looking for servants who had run off with a few items of clothing. They would keep an eye out for Mary Ann Nichols but it wasn't a priority. In Whitechapel, to the officers of H Division, it meant very little indeed. And so Polly settled into the routine of a chronic alcoholic in the poorest, roughest, most dangerous slum that, at that point in history, the world had ever seen.

A jolly bonnet

Three months later, at 12.30 a.m. on Friday, 31 August 1888, Polly was seen leaving the Frying Pan pub in Brick Lane (the stone front of which can still be seen today). Half an hour on, she was sitting in the kitchen of the dosshouse at No. 18 Thrawl Street, wearing a new black bonnet and begging with the deputy to let her stay inside by the fire a while longer. But he was adamant. She didn't have the 4*d* for a bed, but clearly had enough money to go drinking. He chastised her for her misplaced priorities and told her to leave.

Drunkenly she replied: 'I'll soon get my doss money. See what a jolly bonnet I've got!'

Polly was short, overweight and dressed in filthy rags. She had a scar running down her forehead and five of her front teeth were missing. It must have been an amazing bonnet.

Kicked out, Polly went into the narrow, muddy alley that was Thrawl Street, no doubt intending to raise the 4*d* the only way she knew how. It was 1.20 a.m. and she was too drunk to feel the cold night air. She was putting a lot of faith in the pretty bonnet to get her noticed before the many other prostitutes walking the streets, but get her noticed it certainly did.

Emily Holland

A little over an hour later, she bumped into Emily Holland, one of the girls she shared a room with. Emily would later tell the police she had seen her friend just around the corner from the dosshouse at the junction of Brick Lane and Osborn Street. She went on to say that her friend had been very drunk and had not wanted to return to the room despite Emily urging her to. She said Polly had actually boasted to her:

> I've had my lodging money three times today an' I've spent it.
> It won't be long before I'm back.

The implication was that with the new bonnet she couldn't fail to attract a man. She was right.

The time was 2.30 a.m.

B Division

In 1888 the Metropolitan police force was responsible for maintaining law and order in London and they had a full-time job on their hands. In an age before fingerprints, blood groups or forensics, the best they could hope for was to catch a crook red-handed. To this end there were divisions of policemen pounding the beat all over London and in Whitechapel it was the officers of H Division who were the men on the ground. They each patrolled a designated beat, with their areas overlapping, which meant they were never more than a few minutes away from another officer. Armed with their lanterns, truncheons and whistles, they patrolled the streets to differing degrees of competency. Any crime they discovered was followed by frantic whistle blowing that would alert anyone in the vicinity to raise the alarm. Whistles were used because the shrill note travelled further, especially at night. Everyone knew how the system worked and when the whistles started blowing an officer or a civilian would report, usually at high speed, to the nearest police station. Word of what was occurring would then quickly spread from the station.

Buck's Row

Close to where Emily and Polly had exchanged words, no more than a few minutes walk to the east, was a street now called Durward Street and then called Buck's Row. It ran behind and parallel to Whitechapel rail terminus and contained cottages and a school down one side with warehouses serving the goods trains down the other side, nearest the tracks. By day Buck's Row was a busy, thriving thoroughfare, full of people, traffic and noise. But at night the school and the warehouses were closed and the people were sleeping. Then Buck's Row was quiet as a mouse.

At 3.15 a.m. on 31 August 1888, only forty-five minutes after Polly had spoken to Emily, PC John Thain passed one end of Buck's Row on his designated route in his usual manner. He looked down the road but saw nothing to cause him suspicion or alarm. He kept moving. At almost the same time, within a minute or two, PC John Neil walked down the whole of Buck's Row whilst covering his beat. He also saw nothing out of the ordinary and described the scene as quiet, normal. Later both officers would be specific in their times.

A resident of one of the cottages, Harriet Lilley, later told a reporter that she thought she might have heard a noise at around 3.30 a.m. but as she lay in bed trying to place the sound a train passed by and she gave up listening and went back to sleep.

The body

At 3.40 a.m. George Cross, a cart driver at Pickford's Removals, entered Buck's Row on his way to work. Dawn had started to break: the blanket of night becoming a series of separating shadows, the sky growing lighter by the minute. As he walked down the street Cross noticed an unusual shape in what appeared to be a slight recess on his left-hand side.

Between the cottages and the school he saw a shadowy bundle lying on the ground. Cross was by no means a wealthy man and he

'Polly' Nichols found by
PC John Neil. (THP)

crossed to the shape, possibly thinking it might be a large sheet of tarpaulin or something of use or value.

The recess was a locked gateway leading to some stables and the tarpaulin, he realised as he drew closer, was a woman lying on her back.

George Cross stopped in his tracks and listened intently. He was not sure if anyone else might be close by. He could hear no horses or wagons.

But then he heard footsteps

Robert Paul, also a cart driver, was on his way to an early start at work when he saw Cross crouched over in the gateway. He started to cross the road to avoid the stranger, when Cross touched him on the shoulder. 'Come and look at this woman,' he said.

Both men thought the woman had been attacked and raped. Her skirt was still up around her waist and Paul adjusted it to preserve her dignity. Paul, thinking she was drunk, wanted to try and lift her to her feet, but Cross disagreed. Paul later testified that he thought he detected a movement as though she was breathing. The men decided it was best to leave her and try to find a policeman.

A couple of minutes later, PC Neil came back into Buck's Row. Unlike the two men who had just hurried off for help, the officer had a lantern. He was able to see immediately that the victim's throat had been viciously cut wide open and blood was coming from her neck, soaking into her clothing. PC Neil felt her hands for body warmth; judging by her temperature he thought the woman had only just been killed.

As he was kneeling over her, checking for a pulse, the movement of his lamp attracted PC Thain, whose beat had also brought him back to the scene of the crime. Meanwhile, the two men who originally discovered the body returned with another policeman, PC Mizen, and then went on to work.

Fetch a doctor

Thain went to fetch a doctor. Within fifteen minutes a Dr Llewellyn was at the scene. As Thain and Neil shone their lights for him, the doctor examined the woman. Mizen was despatched to Bethnal Green Police Station to get an ambulance.

Dr Llewellyn discovered what they all already knew; her throat had been cut from ear to ear. The wound was so deep it was open all the way through to her backbone. He ordered the unidentified corpse to be taken to the nearest mortuary, where she waited while the two mortuary attendants had breakfast, before they stripped her of her clothing and a policeman listed her few pathetic possessions.

It was now that it was discovered the dead woman had more wounds.

Llewellyn was hurriedly called to the mortuary where he examined her further and discovered bruising and marks around her throat, as though she had been grabbed or punched. He also carefully noted several stab wounds in the area of her stomach and abdomen, including one long cut that had ripped her stomach open.

Llewellyn was not the first person that evening to think that the killer had been disturbed before he'd had a chance to carry out his horrific attack to the fullness of his desires. It was a complete mystery how nobody had seen or heard anything. This was the point at which Jack the Ripper's ability to slip away like a ghost, like a creature of the night with special powers, was first raised.

Meagre possessions

The authorities needed to identify the unfortunate woman. However, her possessions left little to go on. She had been carrying a little broken pocket mirror so they assumed that she was living in a

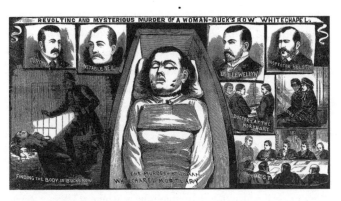

The Buck's Row victim. (© *The Illustrated Police News*, 1888)

dosshouse, where mirrors were considered luxury items. Then they discovered that one of her petticoats had 'Lambeth Workhouse' stamped inside it so they sent an officer there to see if they could find anyone who might be able to help with the identification.

Over the next few days several women came forward hoping to put a name to the body. Among them was an inmate from the Lambeth Workhouse and Polly's roommate Emily Holland. Both declared that, without any doubt, the poor dead woman was Mary Ann 'Polly' Nichols. She was formally identified by her father who testified at the inquest the day after her murder.

This is considered by many Ripperologists to be the first of Jack the Ripper's 'Canonical Five' victims.

The inquest

Her inquest was opened on 1 September amidst much interest from press and public and a large crowd had to be held back from the hall. Three witnesses were called to give evidence on the first day, with eight more waiting. The inquest was reconvened on 17 September and at the end of the second day it was clear there was still much confusion, so proceedings were adjourned again until 22 September to allow the police time to gather more evidence.

By the last day of the inquest another murder had been committed. The coroner, Wynne Baxter, had to concede that it looked to have been committed by the same culprit with the same weapon.

Although the name 'Jack the Ripper' had not yet been invented, people in the East End were starting to get nervous. By drawing attention to the possible connection at the inquest, the coroner was reinforcing the idea that there might be a maniacal killer prowling the streets. Never before had the police known anything like it – somebody was murdering for no apparent reason.

Poor Polly

On 6 September 1888, Mary Ann 'Polly' Nichols was buried at the City of London cemetery. The location of her grave is marked today with a commemorative plaque provided by the council. Her eldest son, who was then 22 years of age, attended the funeral, as did the man she had married in Fleet Street so many years ago and never divorced, William Nichols.

Polly was a product of her environment. She lived in an age when there was no such thing as the NHS, Social Security Benefits or Health and Safety Laws, and where rehab for alcohol addiction had not even been invented. It was a time when the vast majority considered that the poor should 'pull themselves together' and thought people from places like the East End only got what they deserved. Sweatshop owners and slum landlords were allowed to get rich on the back of the misery of others; London had doubled in size in twenty years and things were moving too fast for everybody to keep up.

Polly was an unfortunate who slipped through the cracks and was a victim of a terrible murder. Yet she was far from unique: there were thousands of women in the same situation as her at that time in that place, nearly all forgotten now. Polly, however, lives on. Strangely, the way she died has meant that she will never be forgotten.

George Cross

As something of a footnote, George Cross called himself Charles Cross at the inquest, although one or two newspapers incorrectly reported this as George Cross. However, recent investigations by Ed Stow would suggest that in fact his name was Charles Lechmere!

2

Annie Chapman: The Terror Continues

Clare Smith

John Davis of No. 29 Hanbury Street rose at 5.45 a.m. on Saturday, 8 September for a day's work at Leadenhall Market. After a cup of tea he went into the yard behind the house, and *The Times* reported his words to the inquest of what happened next: 'He saw the

The scene of the crime, No. 29 Hanbury Street.

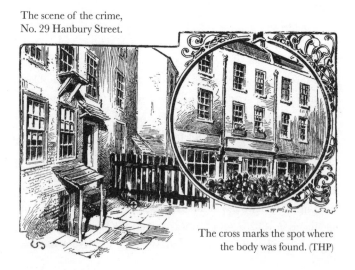

The cross marks the spot where the body was found. (THP)

deceased woman lying flat on her back.' This rather understates his experience, as he had found the body of Annie Chapman, the second canonical victim of Jack the Ripper.

Annie Chapman was also known as Dark Annie, Emily Annie and Annie Sievey/Siffey but was born Annie Eliza Smith. Annie was 47 years old when she was murdered. She was 5-foot tall with dark wavy hair and blue eyes, stout or well proportioned, and the doctor who examined her body stated that she had very fine teeth.

Born in 1841, she was the eldest child of five born to George Smith and Ruth Chapman. In 1869, Annie married John Chapman, a distant relative on her mother's side. John was a coachman and after the marriage he and Annie lived in Bayswater. In 1870, Annie returned to her mother's home in Knightsbridge to give birth to her first child, Emily Ruth. A second daughter, Annie Georgina, was born in 1873. At this time the family was living just off Berkeley Square as John was coachman to a nobleman living in Bond Street.

Drunken Annie

The year 1880 saw the family move to Clewer in Berkshire, where John was employed as a coachman for Josiah Weeks, a local farm bailiff. It was here that Annie had her last child, a son called John Alfred. It was during this time that Annie's drinking problem became public knowledge: after her murder *The Times* reported that Annie was often seen walking in the neighbourhood drunk and had been held in police custody for public drunkenness, although she was never brought before a magistrate on any charge.

Annie's drinking may have been exacerbated by problems in her family; her son is described as a 'cripple' who was placed in a home and one of her two daughters, Emily, was epileptic and died of meningitis in 1882, aged 12. It was around 1882 that the marriage of Annie and John broke down and Annie left Clewer for London.

John made Annie an allowance of 10s a week (£24 a year), the equivalent wage of a shop girl or housemaid.

While in London, Annie stayed in common lodging houses in Whitechapel and Spitalfields. In 1886, Annie was living in Dorset Street with Jack Sivvey, which was why she was known to some as Annie Sivvey or Siffey. After this relationship ended Annie became involved with Edward Stanley, sometimes known by the nickname 'The Pensioner'.

Amelia Farmer

In 1886, Annie discovered her allowance had stopped. She travelled back to Clewer to find out what had happened and discovered that John had died on Christmas Day of cirrhosis of the liver, which implies John was also a heavy drinker. Annie returned to London, where she now had to earn her living. During the inquest into Annie's death, her friend Amelia Farmer testified as to how Annie earned money after her allowance ceased. Amelia stated that, when sober, Annie was very industrious and would make antimacassars to sell or would buy flowers and matches to resell on the streets.

However, Amelia also stated that she did not believe Annie was very particular about how she made her money and that she would often remain out late at night. Timothy Donovan, the keeper of the lodging house where Annie had been living before she died, said Annie brought men to the lodging house. These testimonies confirmed the view that Annie was working as a prostitute.

A diseased drunk?

There were conflicting reports during the inquest in regards to Annie's drinking. Amelia testified that Annie had a taste for rum and was addicted to drink but that it did not take much to get Annie drunk.

Donovan testified that Annie was sober during the week but got drunk on a Saturday night. The post-mortem indicated that Annie had not taken 'strong alcohol' in the hours before her death. This probably refers to spirits and so she may have being drinking beer.

The last week of Annie's life is very well documented due to the testimony of the people who knew her at the inquest. On Saturday, 1 September, Annie was involved in an altercation in the Britannia Pub with Eliza Cooper which resulted in Annie receiving a black eye and bruise to her chest. Annie spent the Saturday night and the day of Sunday, 2 September with Edward Stanley.

On Monday, 3 September, Amelia Farmer reported she had met Annie who was complaining of feeling unwell. Annie told Farmer she intended to visit her sister and borrow a pair of boots to go hop picking. Thousands of people would travel from London to Kent to earn money assisting the harvest of hops. It is unlikely that Annie did go to Kent as she again met Farmer in Whitechapel on Tuesday, 4 September.

Timothy Donovan saw Annie in the lodging house on Friday, 7 September when she told him she had been in the infirmary;

Dr Phillips. (THP)

however, she was also heard to say she had been to her sisters'. In his testimony to the inquest following Annie's murder, Dr Phillips stated that Annie was suffering from an advanced disease of the lungs and brain which may explain her ill health.

During Friday evening Annie was seen at the lodging house but did leave on several occasions. At 1.45 a.m. Annie left for the final time, asking

Donovan not to let her bed for, although she had no money yet, she would soon be back with it. It was assumed that she was going out to pick up a client.

The last confirmed sighting of Annie alive was of her walking towards Spitalfields church.

Annie Chapman. (© *The Illustrated Police News*, 1888)

Terrible wounds

Annie's body was found by John Davis who raised the alarm to three men who were passing the yard. The men went to find a policeman and by 6.10 a.m. Inspector Joseph Chandler of H Division had been informed of the murder and was en route to Hanbury Street. Chandler was the main police witness at the Chapman inquest but his subsequent police career is less than auspicious. In 1892 he was demoted for being drunk on duty and then retired from the force in 1892; it is Inspector Frederick Abberline who the majority of the public associate with the investigation of Jack the Ripper.

As detailed by Evans and Skinner, Chandler's report of 8 September described the horror of Annie's murder:

> A woman lying on her back, dead, left arm resting on left breast, legs drawn up, abducted, small intestine and flap of abdomen lying on right side, above right shoulder attached by a cord with the rest of the intestines inside the body; two flaps of skin from the lower part of the abdomen lying in a large quantity of blood above the left shoulder; throat cut deeply from left and back in a jagged manner right around the throat.

Chandler summoned the police surgeon, Dr George Bagster Phillips. Phillips arrived at Hanbury Street at 6.30 a.m. and made a preliminary examination of the body. Chandler's report notes that, rather redundantly, Bagster 'pronounced life extinct' and Annie's body was moved to Whitechapel Mortuary.

On 13 September, Phillips gave evidence to the inquest into Annie's death, under the coroner Wynne E. Baxter. The newspapers covered the inquest and reported the witnesses' evidence, although they were initially somewhat thwarted by Phillips. *The Times* reported Phillips' testimony on the 14 September. He detailed the position of the body in the yard, that Annie's face and tongue were swollen, that her throat had been cut and there were bloodstains on the wooden fence in the yard.

What Phillips did not describe were the injuries Annie had suffered. Phillips stated that the body was 'terribly mutilated' but did not go into detail. Instead, *The Times* reported on 14 September 1888 that:

> At this point Phillips said that, as from these injuries he was satisfied as to the cause of death of the women, he thought that he had better not go into further details of the mutilations, which could only be painful to the feelings of the jury and the public. The Coroner decided to allow that course to be adopted.

Phillips identified the cause of death as loss of blood caused by the severance of Annie's throat and stated that breathing had been interfered with prior to death. The bruising that Phillips noted on Annie's throat, along with the swollen face and tongue, indicated that the killer had seized Annie by the throat, causing her to lose consciousness, and then had cut her throat. The mutilations had occurred after death.

This was not the end of Dr Phillips' testimony. On 19 September, Coroner Baxter recalled him and insisted that all the injuries that had been identified during the post-mortem be reported to the court. Phillips was hesitant to comply but did so; *The Daily Telegraph* reported that the coroner noted the presence of women and newspaper messenger boys and it was after they had left the room that Phillips revealed the mutilations to which Annie had been subjected.

The papers

The newspapers did not print the details of the mutilations: on 20 September *The Times* described the evidence as 'totally unfit for publication' while *The Daily Telegraph* used the phrase 'terrible wounds' without going into detail. What the papers did report was that parts of Annie's body had been removed and were not found at the crime scene. The *Daily News* reported that 'important portions of the anatomy were missing' while *The Daily Telegraph* mentioned 'parts of the body which the perpetrator of the murder had carried away with him'. Phillips' report detailed that the uterus, upper portion of the vagina and part of the bladder had been removed completely from the body.

Missing

In addition to the missing body parts, it was noted that Annie's rings (she usually wore three brass ones) were not found. Phillips noted bruising on her fingers that would be consistent with rings being violently removed. The police visited local pawnshops but found no trace of the rings.

It was not the missing rings that were identified as the motive for the murder but the missing body parts, specifically Annie's uterus.

In his summing up of the evidence on the 26 September, Coroner Wynne Baxter informed the jury that he had been contacted by a member of staff from a medical school. This staff member had been approached by an American willing to pay £20 for a specimen of the organ missing from Annie's body – the word uterus was not used. Baxter stated that the knowledge of the demand for such a specimen may be a motive for the crime. He also stated that the murderer had considerable anatomical knowledge and skill which, along with Dr Phillips' testimony that the knife used was very sharp with a thin narrow blade and was similar to that used by doctors for post-mortems, began to construct an image of a killer with medical experience.

The first clue

The police had not been idle in the days that followed the murder. In fact, they believed that they had three clues that could potentially lead them to the killer. The first clue was found near Annie's body: it was an envelope that bore the official stamp of 1st Battalion Surrey Regiment. Inspector Chandler had travelled to the barracks of the regiment, interviewed staff and checked the paybook to see if he could find a soldier with the same initials as those found on the envelope. However, no match could be found as the stationery was mass-produced and sold to anyone, not just those who were part of the regiment. On 15 September, the mystery of the envelope was solved when William Stevens, who had lodged at the same house as Annie, went to police to report that he had seen Annie pick up the envelope from the kitchen floor to use to hold two pills.

The second clue

The second clue came from the statement of Mrs Elizabeth Long, who stated that she had seen Annie in the company of a man at 5.30 a.m. on 8 September in Hanbury Street. Mrs Long heard the man say 'Will you' and the woman answer 'Yes'. Mrs Long was positive that the woman was Annie Chapman but she could not provide a detailed description of the man: all Mrs Long could confirm was that he was wearing a dark coat, was a little taller than Annie and she believed he was a foreigner. In Whitechapel in 1888, foreigner was usually a euphemism for Jewish and could have meant no more than the man was dark haired.

Mrs Long's statement seemed to be supported by that of Albert Cadosch who lived at No. 27 Hanbury Street. Just after 5.30 a.m. Cadosch was in the yard, where the communal toilet

Did Albert Cadosch hear Annie Chapman fall against the fence?
(© *The Illustrated Police News*, 1888)

would have been located, and stated he had heard a woman say 'No' and then the sound of something falling against the fence. Phillips testified that the fence in the yard of No. 29 Hanbury Street was smeared with blood, which could support Cadosch's statement.

Mrs Long's witness statement was not of help to the police as it contradicted the medical evidence provided by Phillips. It was 6.30 a.m. when Phillips arrived at Hanbury Street on 8 September and he believed that Annie had been dead for two hours, which would have put the murder at 4.30 a.m., an hour before the sighting by Mrs Long. During the inquest, Wynne Baxter had suggested that the temperature of the morning and the loss of blood may have caused Phillips to make a mistake about the time of death.

The trail did not lead to an arrest.

The third clue

The third clue was a piece of leather apron that the police had found in the yard. It belonged to the son of Amelia Richardson who testified at the inquest that her son wore it for his work. On Thursday, 6 September, Mrs Richardson had washed the apron and left it in the yard to dry, which is why the police found it at the murder scene. The reason that this was mentioned at the inquest may be connected to the man known as 'Leather Apron' who had been reported as having behaved in a threatening manner to women who worked as prostitutes in the Whitechapel area. Detective Sergeant William Thicke identified the man as John Pizer and on 10 September took him into custody for questioning. Pizer was able to provide alibis for both the murder of Mary Ann Nichols and Annie Chapman.

Conspiracy

The crime scene of Hanbury Street has been the source of one of the most enduring myths of the many that emerged from the Whitechapel Murders in 1888. The myth concerns not only the items found with Annie's body but where they were placed. During the inquest, Inspector Chandler's testimony was that after Annie's body was removed from the yard a piece of coarse muslin and a small pocket comb was found. This was contradicted by the evidence of Phillips who stated that he had found the muslin and the comb, and that they had been placed at the feet of the victim in an ordered or arranged fashion. Who found a piece of muslin and a comb and where they were placed does not seem to be of great importance. However, these objects and their location in regard to Annie's body have taken on significance in the theory of a Masonic/royal plot as the motive for the Ripper murders.

Knight's theory

In 1975 Stephen Knight published *Jack the Ripper: The Final Solution*, a book that claimed to solve the mystery of who Jack the Ripper was and an exposé of the royal conspiracy behind the murders. Knight quoted an 1888 press report in the *Pall Mall Gazette* that not only were the muslin and comb found at Annie's feet but also the rings that Annie wore. There was also a report in *The Daily Telegraph* in 1888 that 2 farthings were found with Annie's body.

These items became part of the evidence for Knight's theory that Jack the Ripper was Sir William Gull, Queen Victoria's doctor, who had murdered the women following Masonic law. Knight highlighted that brass was sacred to Masonic tradition and that before the initiation of a Mason all metals are removed from him – this would include rings and coins. The fact that the police and the coroner stated that Annie's rings were missing was, Knight believed, evidence of police and establishment involvement in a conspiracy to protect Gull.

Burial

The verdict of the jury after the inquest into Annie's death was wilful murder against some person or persons unknown. This remains the case in terms of identifying Annie's killer. On 14 September 1888 at 9 a.m., Annie's body was buried at public grave 78, square 148 at Manor Park cemetery, Forest Gate. The arrangements had been kept secret with only the police and the family being aware of the time and place of burial. Annie's family may have wished to avoid the crowds that had gathered to watch the funeral procession of the first victim, when a police guard was needed to ensure the hearse could reach the cemetery. Murder and the inquest had violated Annie's body and privacy, and her weaknesses – both physical and moral – had been exposed. Her private funeral may have been an attempt to restore some privacy to Annie and her family.

Annie's grave no longer exists as it has been buried over. It is still possible to see the yard of No. 29 Hanbury Street, where Annie was murdered, on film: *The London Nobody Knows* of 1967 shows the actor James Mason walk through the house and into the yard of Hanbury Street, the location little changed since Annie's murder seventy-nine years earlier.

Bibliography

Evans, Stewart P. and Keith Skinner, *The Ultimate Jack the Ripper Sourcebook: An Illustrated Encyclopedia* (London: Robinson, 2001)

Knight, Stephen, *Jack the Ripper: The Final Solution* (London: Harrap, 1975)

The Times
The Daily Telegraph
Daily News

3

Elizabeth Stride:
The Night Of The Double Event

Jacqueline Murphy

Elisabeth Stride was born on 27 November 1843 in Sweden. Her parents were Gustaf Ericsson and Beata Carlsdotter, and they worked on the small farm called Stora Tumlehed, in a village called Torslanda. Elisabeth was christened Elisabeth Gustafsdotter on 5 December in the small village church, which is still standing. She had an elder sister, Anna Christina, and two younger brothers, Carl Bernhard and Svante. Not much is known about her early life, but by 1860 she had moved to Gothenburg to work as a domestic servant for a man called Lars Frederick Olofsson, a workman with four children. Her friends also claimed that she could speak Yiddish.

Elisabeth was registered as a prostitute by the police in March 1865 and in April that year she gave birth to a stillborn baby girl. It is not known why Elisabeth became a prostitute: more money perhaps, less physically tiring than being a domestic maid, or was she even dismissed by her employer for being pregnant? We do know that servants found it difficult to obtain new work without references, especially if pregnant. As a single mother, options were limited and prostitution was often the only way to make ends meet. Later that year she was treated for venereal disease at the Kurhauset hospital. Initially she was treated for genital warts but later for a chancre (a contagious ulcer), which is an early indication of syphilis.

To England

Towards the end of 1865, Elisabeth decided to move to England. On 7 July 1866, she appeared on a Swedish parish register in London as an unmarried woman and started spelling her name as Elizabeth, with a z instead of an s. As Sugden points out, this entry states that she could read tolerably well but possessed only a poor understanding of the Bible and catechism. Begg adds that Elizabeth had recently inherited 65 Swedish krona after the death of her mother and that, on 7 March 1869, she married John Stride before they set up a coffee shop together in Chrisp Street, Poplar. But by the end of 1881 this marriage seems to have broken down.

Elizabeth was admitted to the Whitechapel Infirmary with bronchitis and then discharged to the Whitechapel Workhouse in January 1882. She told people that she was a widow, her husband and children having died in the *Princess Alice* disaster of 1878. This steam ship had collided with another ship, *Bywell Castle*, in the Thames, with over 600 people killed. John Stride was not one of them; he had actually died in October 1884 of heart disease. Elizabeth also claimed that she had nine children, but no record of this can be found.

From 1882 Elizabeth lived at No. 32 Flower and Dean Street, in the heart of Whitechapel. She worked occasionally as a servant, cleaning rooms, and working for the local Jewish people who were unable to work on the Sabbath due to their religious views. In 1885 she started to live with Michael Kidney, a dockside labourer, but the relationship was stormy. Elizabeth often left him, returning to Flower and Dean Street, but after her death Michael claimed she would go away due to drink and that she liked him more than any other man. Elizabeth also collected alms (charity) from the Swedish church on occasions, and probably resorted to prostitution to supplement her small income when needed. During this period the couple lived at various common lodging houses, principally in Devonshire Street, near the river, but also Dorset Street.

Michael Kidney. (THP)

In March 1887, Elizabeth was listed as an inmate of the Poplar Workhouse, and the following month she charged Michael Kidney with assault, but failed to attend the magistrates' hearing to press charges. Kidney was charged with being drunk and disorderly in July 1888 so it seems there may have been faults on both sides of the relationship.

Elizabeth claimed that Michael sometimes locked her in the room when he went out, and in her possession at the time of her death was a padlock key.

At No. 32 Flower and Dean Street.

No. 55, Flower and Dean Street.

No 32, Flower and Dean Street.

(THP)

Long Liz

In September 1888, Elizabeth lived once again in Flower and Dean Street. Here she was known by a variety of names including Annie Fitzgerald, Epileptic Annie, Hippy Lip Annie, Mother Gum and Long Liz. 'A better-hearted, more good natured cleaner woman never lived,' said Ann Mill, a bed-maker at No. 32 Flower and Dean Street. Elizabeth had blue eyes and brown curly hair, and measured 5 feet 2 inches. The nickname 'Long Liz' may be due to her surname, Stride, rather than her height.

On the 25th Elizabeth left Michael Kidney for the last time, telling Catherine Lane, a fellow lodger, that they had had a row, though Kidney later denied this. On Wednesday 26th, the social reformer Thomas Barnardo visited the house. He was asking people about their lives, and the conversation naturally turned to the recent murders. On 6 October, a letter was published in *The Times* in which he recalled the incident, and claimed to recognise Elizabeth as one of the women in the kitchen that day. However, the lodging

Elizabeth Tanner or Turner. (THP)

housekeeper's deputy, Elizabeth Tanner, denied that Elizabeth Stride – 'a very quiet woman' – was there that day, stating she was only there on the Thursday and Friday nights. Another lodger, barber Charles Preston, said Elizabeth had been arrested for being drunk and disorderly. He seemed to know many 'facts' about her, Elizabeth having confided to him the *Princess Alice* story as well as telling him that she had come to England in the service of a foreign gentleman. Preston had lived at No. 32 Flower and Dean House for the past eighteen months, so would have seen Elizabeth whenever she was separated from Michael Kidney.

On the afternoon of Saturday, 29 September, Elizabeth Stride was given 6*d* to clean the lodging-house rooms. At 6.30 p.m. Elizabeth Tanner saw her in the Queens Head public house in Commercial Street.

You would say anything but your prayers

Between 7 p.m. and 8 p.m. Elizabeth Stride had returned to the lodging house and was getting ready to go out. She gave a piece of green velvet to Catherine Lane for safekeeping and tried to borrow a clothes brush from Charles Preston, but he was unable to find it. She wore a black fur-lined jacket, a black skirt, and a black bonnet. The watchman, Thomas Bates, saw her leave, and later said she was 'cheerful'.

At some point that evening, Elizabeth Stride crossed the main Whitechapel Road and headed south towards Commercial Road. At 11 p.m. two labourers, Best and Gardner, entered The Bricklayers Arms, a public house in Settles Street. They saw a woman leave with a man and later stated that they were sure the woman was Elizabeth Stride. Best and Gardner described the man as 5 foot 8 inches, with a thick black moustache, dressed in a black morning suit and a black billycock hat: 'respectably' dressed. He said they went south towards Commercial Street and Berner Street.

As Stride and the man left, Best shouted after them, 'That Leather Apron's going to get you.'

Their destination was less than five minutes' walk from The Bricklayers Arms, but Elizabeth was not seen again until

11.45 p.m. when a man called William Marshall claimed to have seen her in Berner Street. Marshall was standing outside No. 64, on the west side of the street opposite Fairclough and Boyd Streets. He stated that Elizabeth was with a man in a black cutaway coat and a sailor's hat outside No. 63. He said they were 'kissing and carrying on' and he heard the man say to Elizabeth, 'You would say anything but your prayers'. This man in the sailor's hat and the man at The Bricklayers Arms appear to be different men, wearing different clothing. Either Marshall was mistaken about the man's hat and coat or Elizabeth had finished with her first customer and found her second, which could explain the time gap.

Packer

Another witness during this timeframe could be greengrocer Matthew Packer, who lived at No. 44 Berner Street. He saw the body of Elizabeth Stride in the mortuary and identified her as a woman who had bought some grapes for a sixpence with a man at around 11.45 p.m. They then crossed the road and stood for half an hour in the pouring rain before crossing back over the road to stand outside the Berner Street Club (International Working Men's Educational Club). There are several inconsistencies in Packer's evidence.

Initially he told Sergeant White that he hadn't seen anything suspicious or seen anyone standing about in the street. He then told two private detectives, Grand and Batchelor – employed by the Mile End Vigilance Committee – the story quoted above. He later embellished his tale to include a description of the man as being between 30 and 35, of medium height wearing a wide-awake hat and dark clothes. He said the man sounded educated and had the appearance of a clerk. Later still, on 4 October, Packer made a statement to Scotland Yard, this time stating the man was between 25 and 30, wearing a long black coat and a soft felt hat, and now the time is 11 p.m., not 11.45 p.m. Packer also said the man was about 2 or 3 inches taller than the woman. The two witnesses, Packer and Marshall, cannot both be right.

As Packer's initial statement to the police was that he hadn't seen anything, and his later statements 'evolved', I am inclined to disregard his testimony. The height difference between Elizabeth Stride and her companion must have been more than 2 or 3 inches as she was 5 feet 2 inches, and all the descriptions of the man or men seen with her were roughly 5 feet 7 or 8 inches tall. Would the two people stand around in the rain when the public houses were still open? The times stated also change.

Either Matthew Packer was mistaken or a publicity seeker.

Witnesses

The next confirmed sighting of Elizabeth was at 12.35 a.m. A policeman, William Smith, saw her with a young man opposite the International Working Men's Educational Club. Smith described the man as 28 years old, wearing a dark coat and a hard deerstalker hat, and carrying a parcel 6-inches high and 18-inches long that was wrapped in newspaper. He said that they were standing not far from the club but on the opposite side of the road and the woman had a red flower on her coat. Smith later identified Elizabeth in the mortuary as the woman he had

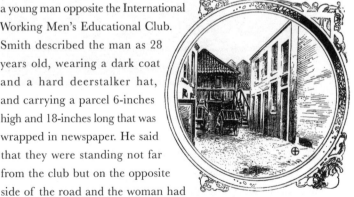

The crime scene in Berner Street. (THP)

Elizabeth Stride enters Dutfield's Yard … (© *The Illustrated Police News*, 1888)

seen. His beat, or route, took about twenty-five to thirty minutes to complete. When he next walked down Berner Street at 1 a.m. he saw a crowd outside the club and went to investigate. Smith made no mention of having seen Elizabeth prior to 12.30 a.m.

The International Working Man's Educational Club was a two-storey building at No. 40 Berner Street. It ran along the north side of Dutfield's Yard and the gates leading to the yard were large and made of wood.

Schwartz

They folded inwards, but the left gate had a small wicket door that allowed access into the yard when the gates were shut. At about 12.45 a.m. a man called Israel Schwartz was walking past this gate when he saw a man stop and talk to a woman. She was standing in the gateway and the man tried to pull her into the street; he then turned her around and threw her to the street. The woman screamed three times, but not very loudly. Schwartz crossed the road and noticed a second man, lighting a pipe. The first man called out, apparently to the second man, 'Lipski'. Schwartz walked away but noticed that the second man was following him, so he ran down to the railway arch but the man didn't follow him that far.

Schwartz was later taken to the mortuary where he identified Elizabeth as the woman he saw. Israel Schwartz's testimony is very interesting. He was a Hungarian Jew and didn't speak English so there may be some error in translation, but he definitely witnessed an assault in the right place, on Elizabeth Stride, at roughly the right time. It is probable that he saw the man who killed her, as it is unlikely that Elizabeth was assaulted twice within ten minutes by two different men.

Schwartz was shaken by the incident: 'Lipski' was a term of abuse towards people of Jewish appearance. The previous year a Jewish man called Israel Lipski was found guilty of murdering a young woman, called Miriam Angel, who was pregnant. The location of the murder was the next street to Berner Street, and there was still a lot of tension regarding this case. Schwartz was unable to say if the two men were together, but neither man came forward later to confirm or deny Schwartz's story.

Other witnesses

No one else could confirm seeing an argument outside the club at that time and there were a few people who would later state they were in the street at around that time. But Schwartz's description of the first man does partly match PC Smith's, although there are some differences. Other witnesses in the street at that time included James Brown, who stated he walked passed a couple, the woman standing with her back to the wall, with the man facing her. Brown heard her say, 'Not tonight, some other night'. Another witness, Fanny Mortimer saw a couple of 'sweethearts' standing for a while in that road. So it could be that Brown and Mortimer saw a different pair, nearer to the junction of Fairclough Street, rather than Elizabeth Stride and her companion. Brown did not see the red flower pinned to Elizabeth's jacket, which she had obtained at some point that evening after leaving her lodging house.

At 12.40 a.m. Morris Eagle, a Russian immigrant jewellery dealer, returned to the Working Man's club having walked a lady friend home. He noticed nothing unusual either when he left at 11.45 p.m. or when he returned. He said it was very dark in the alleyway by the gate though and could not swear that a body was not there. Back inside the club he joined in with the singing when a little while later a man came in saying a body had been found.

Discovery

Just after 1 a.m. a 26-year-old Russian Jew called Louis Diemshultz drove his pony and cart through the gates. His pony shied away as they went through into the dark passage and he looked down at the ground by the right-hand wall and thought he saw a pile of dirt. He prodded it with the end of his whip but it didn't move so he struck a match and saw that it was a woman. At this point Diemshultz thought it was his wife lying drunk, but when he went into the club by the side door he saw his wife there. He then told some people in the club about the woman, so Morris Eagle and a man known as Issacs went out into the yard and saw some blood by the light of a match. They ran out to find the police, Eagle finding PC Henry Lamb and PC Edward Collins. Lamb sent Collins to get the doctor and Eagle to the police station to tell the inspector. He put his hand on the body and found it was still warm. A crowd was gathering by this time and he told them to stand back. At this point PC Smith returned on his beat and saw the crowd. He left to go to the police station to collect the ambulance, a type of handcart, but saw no one as he passed Fairclough Street.

The doctor was asleep, so his assistant Edward Johnson was the first to examine the body. There was a wound to the throat, which appeared to have stopped bleeding. The body was still warm to the touch but the hands were cold. Dr Blackwell then turned up and

Louis Diemshutz finds the body of Elizabeth Stride. (© *The Illustrated Police News*, 1888)

noted the time as 1.16 a.m. He estimated that the woman had been dead around twenty to thirty minutes.

Smeared with blood

Later the inquest would record that Elizabeth Stride was lying lengthwise on her left side, her face completely towards the wall. There was mud on the left side of the face and matted in the hair and the face was pallid with the mouth slightly open. All the teeth on the left lower jaw were absent. The face, neck, chest and legs were quite warm, but the hands were cold. Her feet pointed towards the street and were about 3 yards from the gateway, her legs drawn up and her feet almost touching the wall. Her right hand was lying across her chest and was smeared with blood. It was open. The left hand, lying on the ground, was partially closed and contained a small packet of cachous – a pill used to freshen the breath – wrapped in tissue paper. A number of the cachous were in the gutter. The pocket of the underskirt contained a padlock key, a small piece of a pencil, a pocket comb, a metal spoon, some buttons and a hook.

There was a 6-inch cut in her neck but no other mutilations. The windpipe was completely cut in two but there were no spots of blood on the wall. Her clothing was not wet and there were no grapes in her stomach (disproving Packer's story), just cheese, potato and a farinaceous powder. She had some bruising to her shoulders and on her chest. There were no signs of a struggle, which contradicts Schwartz's testimony. Whilst the doctors were still at Dutfield's yard, police whistles could be heard announcing another murder, a quarter of a mile away, giving this night the sobriquet of 'The Double Event'. However, not all researchers and authors believe Elizabeth Stride was a victim of Jack the Ripper, notably Stewart Evans. Elizabeth was killed with a different knife to the other murders, and there were no other wounds or mutilations.

But others claim that the murderer was interrupted and hiding in the darkness when Diemshultz approached, so he travelled westward to kill again.

Down on her luck

Elizabeth Stride was a well-liked and much respected woman, but down on her luck. She left behind a man who claimed to be devastated by her death, but could he really have been the man who assaulted her in front of the gates? The fact that she screamed not very loudly implies she knew the man and didn't want to make a fuss – or was Schwartz mistaken or lying? There are enough red herrings and witnesses in this particular murder to do Agatha Christie proud. Elizabeth had no money on her when she died. She may have spent her 6*d* at The Bricklayers Arms, but if she did not actively solicit that night what did she do in that time? And if she did, did her killer take her earnings? Berner Street is a small street, now called Henriques Street, not far from the street she lived in when she got married. Did she visit friends? If so, none came forward. It is impossible to believe that she walked aimlessly up and down this tiny street for nearly two hours in inclement weather. She must have been trying to earn some money, especially as she had not paid for her bed in Flower and Dean Street.

Elizabeth Stride was buried at the East London cemetery on Saturday, 6 October 1888.

Bibliography

www.casebook.org
Sugden, Philip, *The Complete History of Jack the Ripper* (Massachusetts: Da Capo Press, 2002)
Begg, Paul, *Jack the Ripper: The Facts* (London: Robson Books Ltd, 2004)

4

Catherine Eddowes: Will It Never Stop?

Mickey Mayhew

The fourth 'canonical' victim of Jack the Ripper, and the second to die in what has been dubbed the 'Double Event', was Catherine Eddowes.

Kate Eddowes. (THP)

According to Philip Sugden, at the time of her death she was 'thin and about five feet in height. She had dark auburn hair and hazel eyes.' She was 46 years old when she was murdered, born in Wolverhampton in 1842. One of eleven children, Catherine moved to London when she was young but later returned to her native Wolverhampton to look for work. She met an ex-soldier called Thomas Conway whilst in Birmingham and later returned to London to live with him; she had his initials, 'TC', tattooed on her forearm. They had three children together, a girl and two boys. Catherine took to drink, part of the pattern so familiar to victims of Jack the Ripper, and by 1880 she had separated from Conway and was living with a new partner called John Kelly at a lodging house in the East End's notorious Flower and Dean Street.

John Kelly. (THP)

Forced to prostituion

Like so many other women living in the area, Catherine was forced to prostitution in order to make ends meet. In Ackroyd's *Jack the Ripper and the East End*, Louise Jackson said, 'the East End was widely associated with prostitution, Whitechapel Road being likened by W. Goldman to an "open-air brothel"'. Paley points out that Kelly, 'when he could … jobbed about the East End markets, while Eddowes, for her part, hawked things in the streets, and sometimes did cleaning jobs for some of the Jewish families'. Again, like so many others living in the area, they would break from the monotony of life in the East End to go hop picking in Kent during the summer months, as they did in 1888. Ripperologist Paul Begg illustrated the popularity of this pastime, 'in 1890 it was estimated that between 50,000 and 60,000 people went to pick hops in a good season'. The season wasn't particularly successful that year and they were back in the East End by the afternoon of Friday, 28 September, having walked most, if not all, of the way back. That night they separated but agreed to meet the following day, and Catherine took a bed in the casual ward at Shoe Lane. It was here that she made a cryptic remark: she was going to earn the reward money on offer because she knew who Jack the Ripper was. No explanation has ever been given for this statement, but it has fed countless conspiracy theories over the years which tie in with the various aliases Eddowes used during the time of her arrest the following day.

The next day Eddowes went to visit her daughter in Bermondsey to try and cadge some money from her. She seems to have attempted to do this on a regular basis, as the daughter, Mrs Annie Phillips, had been wary on previous occasions of letting her mother know where she was living: she had moved around the area several times for this very reason.

Name: 'Nothing'

Whether her mission was successful or not, Eddowes was found later in the day drunk in Aldgate High Street; some sources say she was imitating a fire engine at the time, and had drawn rather a large crowd to watch her antics. Where she got the money from and what she actually did on departing from John Kelly remains a mystery. She was taken into custody by PC Louis Robinson and conducted to Bishopsgate Police Station, where she gave the name 'Nothing' before being detained for the rest of the evening in a cell so that she might sober up.

By 1 a.m. she was released, on this occasion giving her name as 'Mary Ann Kelly of 6 Fashion Street'. It was this seemingly innocent remark, combining the first names of the first canonical victim with the surname of the last that led later conspiracy theorists to connect Eddowes with the fifth and final canonical victim of Jack the Ripper, Mary Kelly (such as Eddowes being killed because she had been mistaken for Kelly). Matters were not helped by the fact that Eddowes sometimes went by the alias of 'Kate Kelly', although there again appears to be no reason to connect this in any way to Mary Kelly.

The sensible explanation was that she simply assumed John Kelly's surname even though they were not married. It is far from impossible that the two women – Catherine Eddowes and Mary Kelly – knew each other, but there appears to be no further connection between the two of them other than the unfortunate one that led to their untimely deaths. Conspiracy theories were further complicated when Eddowes pawned John Kelly's boots in the name of 'Jane Kelly' and with an address of '6 Dorset Street' on the morning of Saturday, 29 September: Jane being the middle name sometimes used by Mary Kelly.

Conspiracy

Perhaps the most famous of all the conspiracy theories is the one put forward by Stephen Knight. In this scenario Eddowes is murdered because she is mistaken for Kelly, for 'when Eddowes was dead the Ripper did not strike again for six weeks. She had called herself Mary Ann Kelly, and the killers thought they had the real Kelly.' Knight suggested that Kelly was the ringleader in a conspiracy of prostitutes to blackmail the government, which was why such extraordinary lengths were gone to in finding and then slaughtering her.

Alan Moore's seminal graphic novel, *From Hell*, has Catherine caught up in the murders because she claims she is Mary Kelly; this work was based loosely around the Knight theory. In the film adaptation of the same name she was played by Lesley Sharp. The title of both the graphic novel and the film refers to the 'From Hell' letter sent accompanied by what was purported to be the kidney cut from Catherine Eddowes' body to George Lusk, head of the Whitechapel Vigilance Committee. In 1988, Michael Caine's Eddowes, in his TV movie *Jack the Ripper*, is played by Susan George.

Goodnight, old cock

Returning to the realms of reality, before Eddowes left the Bishopsgate Police Station, the officer on duty, PC George Henry Hutt, warned her that it was too late for her to get any more drink and that she would be better off getting home before she got into any more trouble. It may seem harsh to modern thinking, to turn a woman out on to the dark streets of London with a serial killer on the loose, but, as Donald Rumbelow points out, 'it was normal policy, and a humane one, to let drunks out when they had sobered up rather than take them to court and punish them with a punitive fine that few of them could pay'.

She said to him, 'Goodnight, old cock,' and then instead of turning right toward Flower and Dean Street and heading for 'home', Catherine Eddowes instead went left, in the general direction of Aldgate, perhaps via Houndsditch. Whichever route she took, by around 1.30 a.m. in the morning she had met Jack the Ripper, who, if the discourse of the 'Double Event' is to be believed, was fresh from murdering Elizabeth Stride a short distance away in Berner Street.

Last sighting

The last known sighting of Catherine Eddowes was by three men, Joseph Lawende, Joseph Hyam Levy and Henry Harris, who had just left the Imperial Club on Duke Street; it was raining, and they had left later than usual as a result. They saw Catherine Eddowes talking to a man at the entrance to Church Passage, which led off Duke Street into Mitre Square, a secluded section bordering the City of London and full mainly of warehouses and just a few residential dwellings.

Mitre Square could be accessed by three different directions: from Church Passage on Duke Street, from the west at Mitre Street,

The last sighting of Eddowes. (THP)

or to the north by St James Passage. The three men didn't linger and saw nothing sinister in the actions of the couple, with Eddowes apparently resting her hand lightly on the man's chest as they talked. Lawende was the only one who took notice of the man, and was later able to furnish the police with a brief description: taller than Eddowes and wearing a cloth cap with a peak. Richard Jones describes how Lawende also saw that the man '... had the appearance of a sailor and was aged about 30. He was around 5 feet 9 inches tall, of medium build, had a fair complexion and a small fair moustache. He sported a reddish neckerchief tied in a knot, wore a pepper-and-salt coloured loose-fitting jacket.' The couple made Levy rather nervous and he remarked to his friends that he didn't like being around at this time of night when there were people like that about.

In later years it would be Lawende who would become the subject of much speculation amongst Ripperologists when it was alleged that he knew who the murderer was but would not name him because the murderer, like himself, was a Jew. These were comments made by Chief Inspector Donald Swanson in Robert Anderson's memoirs, although they have never been verified and neither man actually named Lawende as the man in question.

Mutilation

At around the same time, PC James Harvey walked down Church Passage from Duke Street but his beat meant that he retraced his steps without entering Mitre Square itself, where Catherine Eddowes and her killer may already have been secluded, and where the murder may already have been taking place. The responsibility for patrolling Mitre Square itself fell to PC Edward Watkins, who at 1.45 a.m. discovered the mutilated body of Catherine Eddowes lying in the south-west corner, alongside or in front of the gates that led into the yard of a factory. There was no sign of the murderer, and Trevor Marriot puts forward the notion that 'neither Watkins nor Harvey reported seeing a man pass him or leaving the square hurriedly around the time of the murder. Therefore, presumably, the only route the killer could have taken was the north passage, leading towards the City.'

On peering closer at the corpse, Watkins saw that Catherine Eddowes' face had been horribly scarred.

Paul Begg described how 'the police surgeon believed the mutilation of the face was deliberate. It included nicks to the lower eyelids and two inverted Vs on the cheeks below the eye. The murderer had taken the time to do this.' Her left kidney and part of her womb had been removed, the entrails being slung over her shoulder in a manner almost identical to the murder of Annie Chapman in Hanbury Street. In fact, the mutilations to both face and body were far more severe than those on Chapman, whose face at least the killer had left unmarked. PC Watkins called for assistance to nightwatchman George James Morris, who was an ex-policeman and hadn't seen anything out of the ordinary. Another off-duty policeman who lived near the scene of the crime also failed to see or hear anything suspicious.

On arriving at the scene sometime after 2 a.m., the police surgeon Dr Frederick Gordon Brown declared that Eddowes had been murdered sometime between 1.35 a.m. and 1.45 a.m.

FINDING THE MUTILATED BODY IN MITRE SQARE .

Catherine Eddowes is found in Mitre Square. (© *The Illustrated Police News*, 1888)

The crime scene at Mitre Square. (THP)

He conducted a proper post-mortem that afternoon, during the course of which several photographs of Catherine Eddowes' corpse were taken. These pictures survive to this day: one taken before her

Dr Gordon Browne. (THP)

body was stitched up as part of the post-mortem procedure, and the rest afterwards, wherein she is hooked up to the wall in rather a grisly fashion. Brown believed that the perpetrator of the crime had considerable knowledge of the anatomy in order to carry out the crime, but police physician Thomas Bond disagreed. Bond's opinion was backed up by local surgeon Dr George William Sequeira, who was the first actual doctor at the scene. These were essentially a rehash of the same arguments that had occurred after the murder of Annie Chapman, and which still persist to this day. Martin Fido explains how Sequeira and Dr Sedgwick Saunders, the City Public Analyst, thought that the wounds were the work of 'a completely unskilled ghoul cutting and removing whatever he came across that appealed to him in the abdomen'.

A dirty apron

Not long after the murder was committed a piece of apron was found discarded in a doorway in Goulston Street, not far from Mitre Square, by PC Alfred Long at around 2.55 a.m. The piece of apron was thought to have come from Catherine Eddowes' clothes and was stained with blood and faecal matter; the killer may have cleaned his blade on it before discarding it. It was close to a piece of graffiti found on the wall of a set of apartments called Wentworth Dwellings, and whilst the wording has been somewhat disputed over the years it is generally thought to have said 'The Jews are the men that will not be blamed for nothing', or 'The Juwes are not the men who will be blamed for nothing'. The spelling of the word 'Jews' perhaps as 'Juwes' was meant to have Masonic connotations. Whether or not the killer wrote the graffiti has baffled Ripperologists for decades.

The proximity of the graffiti to the apron may have been complete coincidence, although the wording, with its veiled reference to the Ripper crimes, makes such a coincidence instead seem rather calculated. Perhaps the graffiti was already there and the killer thought it a capital joke to discard the evidence of the crime close by, although one wonders how he might have had the time or the inclination, haring through the darkened streets of Whitechapel. By the same token one must, therefore, also wonder that he had the light and inclination enough to scrawl his cryptic message, however unbalanced he might have been.

The Masonic myth

The message was written down but cleaned off on the orders of Sir Charles Warren, adding more fire to the conspiracy theory claims: Masonic meanings were thought to be hidden in the wording, and with Warren himself a Mason it was thought he was either

Sir Charles Warren ordered the writing to be erased.
(© *The Illustrated Police News*, 1888)

involved or covering up for someone who was. Although the Masonic myth has long lingered, Begg and Bennett dispel it when they say 'washing the writing from the wall did not prevent the spelling of the word becoming known, and as far as we know there was never any attempt made to prevent it from becoming known. All the reasons given for Warren attempting to erase it on the basis of any Masonic connection therefore amount to nothing.'

Inquest and identification

The inquest into Catherine Eddowes' death was opened on the 4 October by Samuel F. Langham, coroner for the City of London. Because of the location of the murder, the City of London police joined the Metropolitan Police in the handling of the investigation, a union out of which considerable friction arose. Among the effects discovered on the corpse was a mustard tin containing pawn tickets, and these were eventually traced back to John Kelly, who had read about the murder in the newspapers. He went to identify the body, as did one of Catherine's sisters, Eliza Gold. Eliza lived in Thrawl Street before Catherine had moved to the area and it may have been her sister's presence there that caused her to make that fateful decision.

As Begg, Fido and Skinner explain, although 'her daughter, Annie Phillips, testified to her scrounging to such an extent that her husband and children deliberately avoided her, others portrayed a more pleasant, if feckless, character. According to John Kelly, Elizabeth Fisher (another sister), Eliza Gold and the deputy at Cooney's lodging house (Frederick William Wilkinson), she was very good natured and cheerful, often singing and rarely drunk.'

After formal identification had been made Catherine Eddowes was buried on Monday, 8 October 1888 in the City of London cemetery in an unmarked grave. All of the expenses of her original burial were met by an undertaker, Mr Hawks. In 1996 a plaque was laid to mark her final resting place, or close to it. Today the site of her murder, Mitre Square, is almost a million miles away in appearance from what it was in the autumn of 1888. As Rob Clack and Philip Hutchinson explain, 'due to its small size, the cobbles on the roadway and the comparative peace and quiet next to so many busy roads, none of the buildings from the time of the Ripper remain. All the

Coroner Langham. (THP)

structures were replaced or removed piece by piece from the 1940s until the 1980s; the spot where Eddowes died, still sometimes referred to as Ripper's Corner, has also been entirely redeveloped. Under the covering arms of a large tree, the spot today is right on the edge of the kerbstones, about two feet from the wall of the school playground.'

Bibliography

Ackroyd, Peter, *Jack the Ripper and the East End* (London: Chatto & Windus, 2008)

Begg, Paul, *Jack the Ripper – The Uncensored Facts* (London: Robson Books, 1988)

Begg, Paul, *Jack the Ripper – The Facts* (London: Robson Books, 2006)

Begg, Paul, Martin Fido and Keith Skinner, *The Complete Jack the Ripper A to Z* (London: John Blake, 2010)

Begg, Paul and John Bennett, *Jack the Ripper CSI: Whitechapel* (London: Andre Deutsch, 2012)

Clack, Robert and Philip Hutchinson, *The London Of Jack The Ripper – Then And Now* (Derby: Breedon Books Publishing, 2007)

Fido, Martin, *The Crimes, Detection & Death of Jack the Ripper* (London: Weidenfeld and Nicolson, 1987)

Jones, Richard, *Uncovering Jack the Ripper's London* (London: New Holland, 2007)

Knight, Stephen, *Jack the Ripper: The Final Solution* (London: Grafton Books, 1977)

Marriot, Trevor, *Jack The Ripper – The 21st Century Investigation* (London: John Blake Publishing, 2002)

Moore, Alan, *From Hell* (London: Knockabout Comics, 1989)

Paley, Bruce, *Jack The Ripper – The Simple Truth* (London: Headline Book Publishing, 1995)

Rumbelow, Donald, *The Complete Jack the Ripper* (London: Penguin Books, 1975)

Sugden, Philip, *The Complete History of Jack the Ripper* (London: Constable & Robinson, 1994)

5

Mary Jane Kelly: The Worst Was Yet To Come

Melanie Clegg

It is one of the greatest ironies of the Whitechapel Murders case that the victim who provokes the most discussion and interest is the one about whom we still know the least. In a way, it is this very lack of knowledge that fuels the fascination with the Ripper's final canonical victim and creates a pervasive aura of mystery around her, but it also underlines the sad near anonymity of the lower classes in this period, the sense that they were a great faceless mass of unwashed and worth less than their more fortunate peers. Would an upper-class woman murdered in Mayfair or even a middle-class housewife from Clapham have remained an enigma for so long? It seems highly unlikely.

In fact, we can't even be sure that Mary Jane Kelly was indeed the real name of this woman, reported to be unusually comely, considering her circumstances, with blue eyes, a fine head of fair hair which fell almost to her

Mary Jane Kelly. Very little is known of her life. (© *The Illustrated Police News*, 1888)

waist, a somewhat stout physique and fresh complexion, and known to be resident at No. 13 Miller's Court throughout much of 1888. After all, it wasn't entirely unheard of for women in dire straits at this time to make use of multiple pseudonyms, often of a rather colourful nature, to cover up their tracks while living on the wrong side of the law or being on the run from difficult personal situations (like abusive fathers, violent husbands, debt, petty crime or trafficking). Certainly, Mary Jane was not the only one of the Ripper's victims that autumn to use an alternative name and we know that she was at various points known as Fair Emma, Ginger or Lizzie Fisher, amongst other nicknames.

However, at some point she had clearly decided on something altogether more humdrum for her everyday life – settling on the distinctly Irish-sounding Mary Jane Kelly, which would suggest that her story about Irish ancestry was indeed true. However, it ought to be remembered that Kelly was a very common surname in the East End of London at the time and had been used as an alias by at least three other possible victims in the Whitechapel Murders (Eddowes, Tabram and Mackenzie), whose own Irish heritage is rather more doubtful.

An enigma

Virtually everything we think we know now about Mary Jane Kelly is gleaned from the testimonies of her former lover, Joseph Barnett, a porter at Billingsgate Market whom she met in 1887. Her actual family has proved impossible to trace despite the efforts of the authorities, police and press. However, we have to take Barnett's information with a hefty pinch of salt as he was clearly infatuated with Mary Jane and was no doubt beguiled by whatever tale she chose to tell him. Naturally, allowance has to be made for Barnett's natural state of shock after being called to Miller's Court on the afternoon of 9 November 1888 to identify the horribly mutilated body of a woman whom he had last seen alive and well the previous evening, and whom it seems likely that he was hoping to be reconciled with one day. However, he did his best despite all of this:

> Her name was Marie Jeanette Kelly. Kelly was her maiden name and the name she always went by. Deceased has often told me as to her parents, she said she was born in Limerick – that she was twenty five years of age – and from there went to Wales when very young. She told me she came to London about four years ago. Her father's name was John Kelly, he was a gauger at some iron works in Carnarvonshire. She told me she had one sister, who was a traveller with materials from market place to market place. She also said she had six brothers at home and one in the army, one was Henry Kelly. I never spoke to any of them. She told me she had married when very young in Wales. She was married to a collier, she told me his name was Davis or Davies, I think Davies. She told me she was lawfully married to him until he died in an explosion. She said she lived with him two or three years up to his death. She told me she was married at the age of sixteen years. She came to London about four years ago after her husband's death. She said she first went to Cardiff and was in an infirmary there for eight or nine months and followed a bad life with a cousin whilst in Cardiff. When she left Cardiff she said she came to London …

It's impossible now to tell how much of this tale is based in fact. Whereas the other victims of the so-called Whitechapel Murderer, despite the relative humbleness of their lives, left quite definite paper trails behind them in the form of census entries, marriage records, birth certificates and entries in infirmary and workhouse registers, nothing like this would seem to exist for Mary Jane. This is despite her appearing to have quite explicitly mentioned a youthful marriage and subsequent widowhood, both events that would have engendered some sort of legal record. In short, despite much effort by researchers, not one single thing from Barnett's account of his ex-lover's life before she met him can be absolutely verified from the available records of the period.

She belonged to the miserable class

However, Barnett isn't the only person to claim some knowledge of the elusive Mary Jane, who seems to have been a well-known and liked personality in the area. A City missionary who worked with the poor of Whitechapel would later claim acquaintance with her in a piece in the *Evening News*:

> I knew the poor girl who has just been killed, and to look at, at all events, she was one of the smartest, nicest looking women in the neighbourhood … I know that she has been in correspondence with her mother. It is not true, as it has been stated, that she is a Welshwoman. She is of Irish parentage, and her mother, I believe, lives in Limerick. I used to hear a good deal about the letters from her mother there. You would not have supposed if you had met her in the street that she belonged to the miserable class she did, as she was always neatly and decently dressed and looked quite nice and respectable.

This tale about Limerick would also be confirmed by Mary Jane's friend Elizabeth Foster and her landlord, John McCarthy, who stated that 'Her mother lives in Ireland, but in what county I do not know. Deceased used to receive letters from her occasionally.'

When it comes to Mary Jane's life in London in the years immediately before her murder, we are on much more certain ground. She gave the impression of being a cut above the average prostitute with her good looks, neat and clean way of dressing, polite manners and relatively high level of education. Certainly Barnett believed that her parents, whom he was admittedly never to actually meet, were 'well to do' (in contemporary terms this could mean anything from being in regular employment to being middle class people of leisure). According to Barnett, Mary Jane had travelled to France, presumably either to work in a brothel there or in the company of a gentlemen who had paid for her services for the trip, but then decided that she didn't like it and abruptly returned to London a fortnight later. At this point, Mary Jane for whatever reason decided not to return to the brothel in the West End where she had been previously working but instead headed to the East End, where she took lodgings with a Mrs Buki who lived on St George's Street, near to the notorious Ratcliffe Highway. This arrangement didn't last long and at some point, according to Joseph Barnett, Mary Jane moved on to different lodgings nearby at No. 1 Breezer's Hill, Pennington Street:

> She was living near Stepney Gas Works. Morganstone was the man she lived with there. She did not tell me how long she lived there. She told me that in Pennington Street she lived at one time with a Morganstone, and with Joseph Flemming, she was very fond of him. He was a mason's plasterer. He lived in Bethnal Green Road. She told me all this but I do not know which she lived with last …

Ex-lovers

Mary Jane Kelly's mysterious ex-boyfriend Morganstone was identified by Neal Shelden and also Evans and Connell in 2000 as a Dutch gas stoker by the name of Adrianus Morgenstern. Adrianus was then tracked down in the 1891 census and found to have changed his surname to Felix and be living in Limehouse with one Elizabeth Felix, who was presumably the same Elizabeth Phoenix who was friends with Mary Jane and who had claimed to the police after the murder that Mary Jane was living with her brother-in-law in Breezer's Hill:

> She stated that about three years ago a woman, apparently the deceased from the description given of her, resided at her brother-in-law's house, at Breezer's Hill, Pennington Street, near the London Docks. She describes that lodger as a woman about 5ft 7in in height, and of rather stout build, with blue eyes, and a very fine head of hair, which reached nearly to her waist. At that time she gave her name as Mary Jane Kelly, and stated that she was about twenty-two years of age, so that her age at the present time would be about twenty-five years. There was, it seems some difficulty in establishing her nationality. She stated first that she was Welsh, and that her parents, who had discarded her, still resided in Cardiff, whence she came to London. On other occasions, however, she declared that she was Irish. She is described as being very quarrelsome and abusive when intoxicated, but 'one of the most decent and nicest girls' when sober … When living at Breezer's Hill, she stated to Mrs Phoenix that she had a child aged two years, but Mrs Phoenix never saw it.

Clearly this brother-in-law was Johannes Morgenstern, Adrianus' brother. In 1885–86 he was living at No. 79 Pennington Street on the corner of Breezer's Hill with a widow called Elizabeth Boeku (Boo-ky). This must surely be the mysteriously monickered Mrs Bucki with whom Mary Jane apparently lodged on St George's Street in the parish of St George's in the East. According to Barnett, Bucki went with Mary Jane to the West End brothel that she had once been a resident of to demand her old dresses and belongings back.

Another ex-lover from this period was Joseph Fleming, who most probably replaced Morgenstern in her affections and who can also be traced with some confidence in the records. He was apparently born in Bethnal Green in the second quarter of 1859 and according to the 1881 census was living in lodgings in No. 61 Crozier Terrace, Homerton, close to Bethnal Green. Recent research would suggest that he was a resident at the Bethnal Green Workhouse for at least some of 1888 so he may have fallen on hard times by that time. He was working as a plasterer in 1881, though, which completely fits with Joe Barnett's account of events, suggesting that although Mary Jane was perhaps fond of embellishing her past background, she was at least relatively honest about her more recent life.

Joseph Barnett

When this living arrangement came to an end, Mary Jane took herself off to new lodgings in Thrawl Street, until she met Joseph Barnett on Commercial Street. After just two meetings in local pubs she decided

Dorset Street. Miller's Court, where Mary Kelly was murdered, is on the left by the carriages. (THP)

to move in with him, first at George Street before moving on to Paternoster Row and Brick Lane before finally settling in a small room in Miller's Court (just off Dorset Street) in the spring of 1888.

Unfortunately, Joseph lost his job at Smithfield Market in the summer of 1888. This inevitably led to some tensions between the couple, particularly when Mary Jane returned to prostitution in order to make some money.

Barnett also testified that, in the months before her death, Mary Jane had become fascinated by the murders happening in their area (which is understandable enough) and that she frequently asked him to read newspaper reports about them to her.

However, he also said that she had been frightened of some unknown person, whom he would later extrapolate could have been the murderer, although she never seems to have actually said so to him.

The couple rowed, probably about money and Mary Jane's return to prostitution, and during the course of one of these arguments the window of Mary Jane's room was broken. In the end, it all proved too much for Barnett and he left her on 30 October, later telling police that 'I left her because she had a person who was a prostitute whom she took in and I objected to her doing so – that was the only reason'.

Joseph Barnett was to see Mary Jane Kelly alive for the last time on the evening of 8 November. Although the couple had separated and, to all intents and purposes, gone their separate ways a week earlier, he still visited and gave her money. After he left, Mary Jane headed out to the Horn of Plenty pub on the corner of Dorset Street with friends and was seen by another Miller's Court residence, fellow prostitute Mary Ann Cox, coming home with a client at around 11.45 p.m., after which she was heard singing in her room between 12 a.m. and 1 a.m.

All was silent

George Hutchinson, a local drifter who knew Mary Jane well, claimed to spot her out and about again at 2 a.m. on Commercial Street. He told the police that she stopped him near Flower and Dean Street and asked if he could give her 2*d*, which he was unable to do. After this he saw her pick up another man and make her way back with him towards Dorset Street. This wasn't a very out of the ordinary thing for Mary Jane to do, of course, due to her profession. However, Hutchinson claimed that there was something about the man that he didn't like. He described the man as being in his mid-30s, about 5 feet 6 inches tall, dark haired, pale complexioned, wearing a long, dark, astrakhan collared and cuffed coat and of being respectable and rather 'Jewish' in appearance. This made him turn back and follow them to her lodging. He then proceeded to lurk opposite the entrance to Miller's Court until around 2 a.m., at which point he gave up waiting for either Mary Jane or the mysterious client to come out and went on his way.

"HE TURNED AND LOOKED AT ME."

The suspicious man in the lined coat. (THP)

Around an hour later, Mary Ann Cox, who had been coming and going all night, returned to her room and noted that there was no light showing from Mary Jane's room and that all was silent. However, about half an hour after this, two other residents of Miller's Court, Elizabeth Prater and Sarah Lewis, heard a female voice crying 'Murder' but apparently thought nothing of it and went back to sleep. It was quiet from then on until around 5.45 a.m. when Mary Ann Cox apparently heard someone, possibly the murderer, leaving the court.

Confusingly two other witnesses, Caroline Maxwell and Maurice Lewis, would later come forward and claim to have seen Mary Jane out and about around the Britannia pub on the corner of Dorset Street, the next morning, at 8.30 a.m. and 10 a.m. respectively. This casts some doubt on the traditional chain of events, which has Mary Jane being murdered at around 4 a.m. and the body lying undiscovered until the late morning. However, the medical evidence for the time of death, which was based on the Victorian understanding of how rigor mortis works and a study of the food remaining in the victim's intestines (in this case a final meal of fish and potatoes), suggests that it could possibly have taken place anywhere between twelve and six hours before the examination at around 1.30 p.m., which means that perhaps Maxwell was correct and Mary Jane was actually murdered much later in the morning than is generally supposed. Sadly, the lengthy delay in gaining admittance to her room, and the somewhat sketchy science of the times, means that the truth of when she was actually murdered will never be known.

The morning of 9 November dawned bright and breezy and the streets were already busy at dawn as it was the day of the annual Lord Mayor's Parade. This splendid pageant through the streets of London was a favourite treat of the City's East End population, who turned out in force to see the Lord Mayor's gilt-encrusted coach go past. However, on this occasion, Mary Jane's landlord John McCarthy had other thoughts on his mind – Mary Jane had

THE AWFUL DISCOVERY BY McCARTHY.

The terrible sight of Kelly's body was first seen through her window.
(© *The Illustrated Police News*, 1888)

fallen several weeks behind with her rent and he had had enough.
He therefore sent one of his men, a Thomas Bowyer, round to
Miller's Court at around 10.45 a.m. to collect what he could.

Bowyer first of all knocked on Mary Jane's door and then, when she
failed to answer, peered through the broken windowpane. He recoiled
in appalled horror from the sight that met his eyes. He then went to
find McCarthy and brought him back to take a look before they went to
Commercial Street Police Station to report the crime. They returned
with the desk inspector on duty, Walter Beck. It wasn't until 1.30 p.m.,
however, after a lot of fruitless waiting for a pair of bloodhounds with
which the police hoped to track the killer's scent, that the door, which
had been locked at the latch via the cracked window, was broken down
and people were able to enter Mary Jane's room for the first time.

What they were to see there was to stay with them forever.

Breaking down Kelly's door. (THP)

Extensive mutilations

The divisional police surgeon, Dr Phillips, had been on the scene since 11.15 a.m. and was one of the first to enter the room. He hastened to examine the body and give his initial opinion on the manner of death (having already taken a look through the broken window upon arrival to ascertain that there was no chance she might still be alive). He first confirmed that the neck had been deeply slashed, which was the probable cause of death, with the extensive mutilations occurring post-mortem. He then went on to detail the treatment of Mary Jane's body, which included the removal of her face and breasts and the skinning of her thighs and abdomen, the contents of which littered the room and around her body. There were also deep jagged cuts on her arms, one of which had been partially separated from the body, and what may have been an attempt to remove her head as well. As was the pattern with the Ripper murders, the killer – after taking full advantage of the time and privacy to do as he pleased with his victim – appeared to have taken a grisly trophy.

Her heart was recorded as 'absent'.

The medical examination of Mary Jane's corpse *in situ* took almost two and a half hours, after which it was removed in a covered van and taken to the Shoreditch Mortuary in the grounds of St Leonard's church. There the body was reconstructed as much as possible, a lengthy task that involved returning the organs to their original positions and possibly also stitching the face together again, before another, more detailed, post-mortem was carried out. Although rumours linger that Mary Jane was pregnant at the time of her murder, there is no medical evidence to support this.

The inquest took place at Shoreditch Town Hall on 12 November. The coroner, Roderick MacDonald, took less than half a day of evidence from Barnett, Dr Phillips and others involved in the case to come to his not-at-all surprising conclusion: the unfortunate young woman's death had been the result of wilful murder at the hands of some person or persons unknown.

The remains of Mary Jane Kelly were taken from Shoreditch Mortuary on 19 November, ten days after her murder, and driven to St Patrick's Catholic cemetery in Leytonstone. They were interred in an unmarked grave in front of a large crowd of mourners. As was the case with the other Ripper victims, the streets of Spitalfields were thronged with people of all ages who watched in silent respect as the funeral cortège made its way through the area.

6

Were There Other Victims?

Robert Clack

There are eleven victims in the Scotland Yard files relating to the Whitechapel Murders. Not all eleven murders were committed by the same hand and only five of the victims, known as the Macnaghten Five, are generally accepted to be victims of Jack the Ripper.

The other six murders may or may not have been committed by Jack the Ripper. However, a case could be made for some if not all to be included in the killer's total.

The six other victims are:

Emma Elizabeth Smith

Very little is known of Emma's life. What we do know is that she was a 45-year-old widow and had a son and daughter living in the Finsbury Park area of London. Since November 1886 she had been living in a lodging house at No. 18 George Street, Spitalfields and her usual habit was to leave home around 6 p.m. or 7 p.m. and return at any hour, usually drunk. According to the lodging housekeeper,

Mary Russell, Emma acted like a mad woman when drunk and had once been thrown through a window.

At 12.15 a.m. on Tuesday, 3 April, Emma was seen by a fellow lodger, Margaret Hames, talking to a man wearing black clothes and a white scarf near Burdett Road, Limehouse. Margaret Hames was hurrying away from the area, as she had been assaulted by some young men a few minutes before. Hames did not think the man talking to Emma was one of them.

Just over an hour later, at 1.30 a.m., Emma was walking alongside Whitechapel church when she saw three men coming towards her. She crossed the road to avoid them and walked along Osborn Street. The men followed her and as she passed the corner of Brick Lane and Wentworth Street she was robbed of all her money and viciously assaulted by the men. Her head was bruised, her right ear torn and bleeding, and a blunt instrument brutally thrust into her vagina, tearing her peritoneum.

Osborn Street, Whitechapel, where Emma Smith was attacked. (THP)

Severely injured from the attack, it took Emma over two and a half hours to stagger back to her lodgings, which were only 300 yards away. Mary Russell and fellow lodger Annie Lee immediately took Emma to the London Hospital where she was seen by Dr George Haslip. Emma had been drinking but was not intoxicated, and she told him what had happened to

The coroner, Mr Wynne Baxter. (THP)

her. She denied she was soliciting and she could not say whether a knife was used on her. Emma could not describe the men who had attacked her, but one of them, she believed, looked about 19. Emma's condition slowly deteriorated and she died the following morning at 9 a.m. A post-mortem found that the cause of death was the injuries to the perineum, the abdomen and the peritoneum. In his words, great force must have been used and the injuries set up peritonitis, which resulted in Emma's death.

Shockingly, the police were not called, and only found out about Emma's death when the coroner's officer informed them on Friday, 6 April that an inquest would be held the following day. Local Inspector Edmund Reid headed the enquiries into Emma's murder. All the constables on duty in the area were questioned but none had seen or heard anything and the streets were said to be quiet at the time.

Vicious assaults were common but the extreme violence suffered by Emma Smith was very unusual and it was commented on by Coroner Wynne Baxter, who said during the summing up of the inquest into Emma's death that:

From the medical evidence it was clear that the woman had been barbarously murdered. Such a dastardly assault he had never heard of, and it was impossible to imagine a more brutal case.

The jury returned a verdict that would become all too common:

Wilful murder against some persons unknown.

Martha Tabram

At about 4.45 a.m. on the morning of Tuesday, 7 August 1888, John Saunders Reeves, a waterside labourer, was leaving his home at No. 37 George Yard Buildings in search of work. As he was passing the first-floor landing he saw a woman lying on her back in a pool of blood. Her arms were by her side, the hands clenched upwards. Her clothes had been torn and disarranged and the bosom of the dress had been torn away. It looked as if she had been in a struggle with someone and there were bloody marks on the landing. No knife or weapon could be seen, and there were no footprints on the staircase. Reeves made his way into George Yard where he found PC Thomas Barrett 226H and told him of his awful discovery. A post-mortem revealed that the woman had been stabbed thirty-nine times in the neck, body and private areas. Time of death was estimated at around 2.30 a.m.

The body was identified as that of Martha Tabram, born Martha White on 10 May 1849 in Southwark, London. She married Henry Samuel Turner on Christmas Day 1869. They had two children together but Martha liked the drink a bit too much and they separated in 1875.

The last few weeks of her life she had been staying at No. 19 George Street, a common lodging house situated right next door to where Emma Smith had lived. While living there Martha went by the name 'Emma'.

Martha Tabram, found stabbed thirty-nine times in George Yard
Buildings. (THP)

Last sighting

On the evening of Bank Holiday Monday, 6 August 1888, Martha
was in the company of Mary Ann Connelly, known as 'Pearly
Poll'. They spent the time from 10 p.m. to 11.45 p.m. drinking in
various public houses in Whitechapel in the company of two soldiers,
a private and a corporal. At 11.45 p.m. Martha and Pearly Poll
parted company; Martha went up George Yard with the private and

Pearly Poll went up Angel Alley with the corporal. It would be the last time Pearly Poll saw Martha alive.

There were no sightings of Martha from the time Pearly Poll left her until her body was discovered. At 1.40 a.m. Elizabeth Mahoney returned home with her husband to No. 47 George Yard Buildings. She immediately went out again to buy food for supper and returned within five minutes. Neither Elizabeth nor her husband saw Martha's body, but it was so dark on the stairs that the body could have been there without them seeing it.

The last sighting of Martha, drinking with soldiers. (THP)

At about 2 a.m. a private of the guards was seen by PC Thomas Barrett 226H in George Yard. The guardsman said he was waiting for his mate, who had gone away with a girl. Alfred Crow, living at No. 35 George Yard Buildings, passed the landing at 3:30 a.m. on his way home. He saw a figure lying on the staircase, but since it was not an unusual sight he did not investigate further.

Pearly Poll and PC Barrett failed to identify the soldiers they had seen at an identity parade held at the Tower of London. It was discovered that the soldiers Pearly Poll had seen belonged to the Coldstream Guards. An identity parade was held at Wellington Barracks where she picked out two men, but both had alibis for the night in question.

With no further witnesses or evidence forthcoming, the investigation into Martha Tabram's death reached a standstill. The conclusion of the inquest was the now-familiar verdict of death by person or persons unknown.

Catherine Mylett

Listed in the Official Whitechapel Murder files as 'Rose Mylett alias Lizzie Davis', Mylett, born on 8 December 1859 in Whitechapel, was actually called Catherine. By 1880 she was living with Thomas Davis, a commercial traveller, and they had at least two children together. They parted around 1885 and she went to live in various lodging houses, the last being No. 18 George Street.

At about 8 p.m. on Wednesday, 19 December 1888, Catherine was seen speaking with two sailors in Poplar High Street, near Clark's Yard. She had the appearance of being sober and was heard saying 'No, no, no!' to one of the men. She was next seen at 2.30 a.m. the following morning, outside The George Tavern in Commercial Road, drunk and in the company of two men.

Shortly before 4.15 a.m. Neos Green was in Poplar High Street when she saw two men she believed to be sailors hurrying towards her.

They asked her the way to West India Docks. She told them and one of them said 'Make haste, Bill, and we shall be in time to catch the ship.'

At 4.15 a.m. Police Sergeant Robert Golding 26K was patrolling Poplar High Street with PC Barrett 470K. As they were passing the entrance to Clark's Yard, PS Golding found the body of Catherine Mylett. She was lying about 25 feet from the entrance. Her body was still warm, her clothes did not appear disarranged and no mutilation had occurred. She was lying on her left side under a wall, with her head pointing away from the street, left arm lying underneath her, right leg at full length and left leg slightly drawn up. The police initially believed this was a case of accidental death, and that Catherine had leaned against a post which jutted out from the wall, and, having swooned, had fallen and died in the position in which she was found.

Murder?

However, Divisional Surgeon Matthew Brownfield believed this was a case of murder by strangulation. He found a mark on the neck, seemingly made by a cord extending from the right side of the spine round the throat to the lobe of the left ear. He believed the mark could be produced by a piece a fourfold lay cord.

Assistant Commissioner Robert Anderson did not agree with Brownfield and he sent word to Dr Thomas Bond to re-examine Catherine's body. Dr Bond was away and his assistant, Dr Charles Hebbert, went in his place. General Police Surgeon Alexander McKellar also examined the body and both men agreed with Brownfield's opinion. When Dr Bond returned he examined Dr Hebbert's notes and agreed that it was a case of murder.

Assistant Commissioner Anderson was still not satisfied and summoned Drs Bond and Hebbert to express his opinion that this was not a case of murder. Dr Bond went to Poplar to personally examine the body. After his examination he told Anderson that he had changed his mind; he now felt that death had been accidental and that Mylett had fallen down whilst drunk and had choked to death on her stiff velvet collar.

Despite Anderson's pressure on the doctors, the inquest into Catherine Mylett's death returned a verdict of murder by a person or persons unknown.

Alice McKenzie

Alice McKenzie's life was shrouded in mystery. She was said to have been born in Peterborough, Cambridgeshire around 1849, came to the East End of London about 1875 and was said to have lived with a blind man. In 1883 she met John McCormack in Bishopsgate and they lived together at various lodging houses for the next six years. In July 1889 they were staying at Mr Tenpenny's lodging house at No. 52 Gun Street where Alice was known by the nickname of 'Clay Pipe Alice' because she was a habitual pipe smoker.

On the afternoon of Tuesday, 16 July 1889, John McCormack gave her 1s 8d (the 8d was to pay for their lodgings that night). They had an argument and Alice left without paying for the lodgings. She spent the evening in the company of a little blind boy named George Dixon in a public house near the Cambridge Theatre, Commercial Street. While in the public house, Alice fell into conversation with a man and she asked him to treat her to a drink and, after taking George back to the lodging house, she returned to the public house.

At 11.40 p.m. Alice was seen hurrying down Brick Lane towards Whitechapel by Margaret Franklin, a friend of fifteen years. Franklin asked Alice how she was and Alice replied, 'All right. I can't stop now.'

Just after 12.45 a.m. the next morning, PC Walter Andrews 272H was patrolling Castle Alley when he came across the body of Alice McKenzie. She was lying on the pavement close to the Whitechapel Baths. Her skirts had been lifted, exposing superficial mutilations to the abdomen and blood was still flowing from two stab wounds in the left side of the neck. The two wounds dragged slightly forward, and were made from left to right. A wound 7-inches long ran down her right side to her navel, with several scratches beneath, pointing towards her genitalia, which had been nicked at the top.

When her body was removed to the Whitechapel Mortuary a bronze farthing and a clay pipe were found underneath her.

Several arrests were made in connection with the murder of Alice McKenzie but no charges were made against any person and they were released.

The day after the murder, William Brodie walked into Leman Street Police Station and confessed to the murder of Alice McKenzie. He was very drunk. He also claimed to have committed nine other murders in Whitechapel. It was soon established Brodie was of unsound mind and it was advised that he should be charged with the murder of Alice McKenzie to keep him in custody. Before

The corner of Whitechapel High Street and Leman Street, where William Brodie handed himself in, in the late nineteenth century. (© THP)

long it was discovered that he had been in bed at his lodgings in the Strand at the time of McKenzie's murder and he was released. He was soon rearrested for fraud in King's Cross.

The Pinchin Street Torso

At about 5.25 a.m. on Tuesday, 10 September 1889, PC William Pennett 239H was patrolling the north side of Pinchin Street. As he walked towards Back Church Lane he began to cross to the southern side when he noticed, in a railway arch belonging to the Whitechapel Board of Works, what he thought was a bundle. The bundle had not been there when he had passed just before 5 a.m. It turned out to be the body of a woman, but with her head and legs missing. The body was lying on its front and was naked, except for two or three pieces of rag.

A search of the arches was made and three men were found. They were arrested but once the police were satisfied they had no connection to the body they were released.

The woman was of stoutish build and dark complexion, about 5 foot 3 inches in height, and between 30 and 40 years of age. The woman had been dead at least twenty-four hours. Besides the wounds caused by the severance of the head and legs, there was a wound 15-inches long through the abdomen. Round the waist was a pale mark and indentation, such as would be caused by clothing during life, and there was bruising on the back and arms which was caused before death.

Identity

A rumour circulated that the remains were those of Lydia Hart, but she turned up a few days later in St George in the East Infirmary. 'Gorgeianna Smith' was adamant that the remains were those of her daughter Rosina who had been missing since the previous

Wednesday, but she too turned up alive. The mother of Emily Barker from Northampton also believed that the remains were of her daughter but, while Emily Barker's fate is not known, her description did not match those of the remains. A Mrs Cornwall who had been missing from her lodging house was also thought to have been the victim and her fate is similarly undetermined.

Cleary

A few days before the discovery in Pinchin Street, a man named John Cleary walked into the offices of *The New York Herald* and informed the night editor that a murder had taken place in Back Church Lane. It transpired that John Cleary's real name was John Arnold, a newsvendor in Charing Cross, and that while walking in Fleet Street a soldier had approached him and said, 'Hurry up with your papers. Another horrible murder in Back Church Lane.' It was never discovered who this soldier was; described as 35 or 36 years old, 5 foot 6 inches, with fair complexion and a moustache. He was carrying a parcel. Nobody was ever arrested in connection with the murder of this unknown woman, nor was her identity ever discovered.

The Pinchin Street Torso is unique in the list of Whitechapel murder victims in that it is unlike the others on the list, and has more in common with another series of murders during the same period commonly referred to as the Thames Torso murders.

Frances Coles

Frances was born in 1859 in Bermondsey, South London. In the early 1880s she worked for a time at a chemist in the Minories, putting stoppers in bottles. The work caused her pain in her knuckles and she eventually left the job. Following this her life descended into one of drink and prostitution.

On 11 February 1891, Frances met up with James Thomas Saddler, a 53-year-old merchant seaman and fireman. They had known each other for about eighteen months and Saddler was a regular client of hers. They spent the next couple of days together, mostly drinking in different public houses in the area. During the evening of 12 February, Frances bought a new hat with money given to her by Saddler and she kept her old one pinned to her dress. They separated between 9 and 10 p.m. after an argument; Saddler had been robbed of his watch and money and accused Frances of not doing anything to help him.

At about 1.45 a.m. Frances was in Commercial Street. She was fairly drunk and was with fellow prostitute Ellen Callaghan. A short man with a dark moustache, shiny boots and blue trousers approached them and asked Ellen to go off with him. She refused and he punched her and tore her jacket. He then asked Frances to go with him which she did, despite Ellen saying to her, 'Frances, don't go with that man; I don't like his look.'

The body

At 2.15 a.m. PC Ernest Thompson 240H was patrolling Chamber Street. Thompson had only been with the Metropolitan Police for two months and this was his first night walking the beat alone. As he was approaching Swallow's Gardens he heard footsteps walking away in the distance. The Chamber Street end of Swallow's Gardens was a railway arch belonging to the London & Blackwall Railway, and Thompson turned into the archway to continue his patrol. About halfway into the arch he came across the body of Frances Coles. Blood was flowing from a neck wound and he shone his lantern into her face. Frances was barely alive; one of her eyes opened and then closed. Thompson blew on his whistle for assistance and help arrived within a few minutes. It was not enough, however, and Frances was pronounced dead at 2.30 a.m.

The victim's throat had been cut twice and there was no abdominal mutilation. Marks on her back suggest that she had either fallen to the ground or was pushed. A search of the archway revealed a folded piece of newspaper containing 2*s* behind a waterspout.

James Thomas Saddler was arrested the next day for the murder of Frances Coles. He was also strongly suspected of being Jack the Ripper. Joseph Lawende, who may have seen Catherine Eddowes with a man shortly before her death, was asked to try and identify Saddler as that man, but failed to do so.

Saddler was seen by Sergeant Edwards 7H at Mint Pavement at about 2 p.m. Saddler was drunk and could hardly walk straight. He had a cut over his left eye and his face was smeared with blood. He told Sergeant Edwards he had just been assaulted. Saddler was next seen trying to gain admittance to No. 8 Whites Row lodging house at 3 a.m. but was refused admittance. With no knife found and no evidence to connect him with the murder of Frances Coles, he was released.

7

The Police

William Beadle

London has two entirely separate police services. The largest, the Metropolitan Police, was founded in 1829 by the then Home Secretary, Sir Robert Peel. Evans details how in 1888 the commissioner was Major General Sir Charles Warren and under him were three assistant commissioners, four chief constables

Much criticism was to be levelled at the police during the hunt for the Ripper. (© *The Illustrated Police News*, 1888)

(now deputy assistant commissioners), thirty superintendents, 837 inspectors, 1,369 sergeants and 12,025 constables.

As Jones explains, the area encompassing the City of London has its own police service. It is the smallest in England and Wales and has only two police stations. The City police was inaugurated in 1839 and in 1888 it was headed by Colonel Sir James Fraser. Fraser was absent throughout the

PUNCH, OR THE LONDON CHARIVARI.—October 13, 1888.

WHITECHAPEL, 1888.

First Member of "Criminal Class." "FINE BODY O' MEN, THE PER-LEECE!"
Second Ditto. "UNCOMMON FINE!—IT'S LUCKY FOR HUS AS THERE'S SECH A BLOOMIN' FEW ON 'EM!!!"

"I have to observe that the Metropolitan Police have not large reserves doing nothing and ready to meet emergencies; but every man has his duty assigned to him, and I can only strengthen the Whitechapel district by drawing men from duty in other parts of the Metropolis."—*Sir Charles Warren's Statement.* "There is one Policeman to every seven hundred persons."—*Vide Recent Statistics.*

Punch cartoon of 13 October 1888, satirising the Metropolitan Police and the criminal classes, and Sir Charles Warren's difficulties finding enough men to catch the Ripper. (THP)

Jack the Ripper murders and the City police were commanded by Chief Superintendent Henry Smith (who succeeded Fraser as commissioner in 1890). Reporting to Smith were one superintendent, fourteen inspectors, ninety-two sergeants and 781 constables.

The onset of the Ripper crimes found the Metropolitan Service beset by many problems. In his annual report for 1887, Sir Charles recorded that of his 14,081 officers only 8,773 were available for 'duties in the street' at any one time, the rest being deployed on special duties, sick or on leave. He pointed out that there were less police available pro rata to protect a populace of 5,476,447 than in 1849, when there were 5,288 officers for 2,473,758 people.

Monro and Anderson

Internally, relations between Warren and his assistant commissioner for crime, James Monro, were poor. In addition to the 800-strong Criminal Investigation (Detective) Department, Monro was also

Home Secretary Henry Matthews. (THP)

head of Department D, a tiny secretive group of detectives who were the forerunner of Special Branch. Warren was outraged that Monro reported directly to the Home Secretary on Department D's activities. Moreover, Monro believed that the CID should also be outside the commissioner's control.

Things came to a head in August. Adolphus Frederick Williamson, the chief constable of the CID, became ill and

Monro wanted to appoint an acquaintance of his, Melville Leslie Macnaghten, as assistant chief constable. Warren objected to Macnaghten and Monro resigned, moving across to the Home Office where he continued to command Department D with the title 'Head of Detective Services'. Robert Anderson, a former Home Office spymaster, took over as assistant commissioner.

Throughout the Ripper murders, Monro and Anderson liaised with each other and with Home Secretary Henry Matthews behind Warren's back.

The Met's hunt for the Ripper

Anderson took up his duties on 1 September but, feeling unwell, left for a period of sick leave the same day that Annie Chapman was murdered. On the 15th, Warren appointed Chief Inspector Donald Sutherland Swanson to take day-to-day control of the investigation into the crimes:

> Swanson must be acquainted with every detail … every paper, every document, every report, every telegram must pass through his hands. He must be consulted on every[thing] … I give him the whole responsibility.

Warren nevertheless stipulated that Swanson should himself consult with Chief Constable Williamson. With the latter's health problems, this meant Swanson liaising with the senior assistant commissioner, Alexander Carmichael Bruce, and Williamson's deputy, Superintendent John Shore.

In the East End, Martha Tabram and Annie Chapman's murders were being investigated by H Division CID under Divisional Inspector Edmund John James Reid (on whom the BBC's *Ripper Street* is based), while that of Mary Ann Nichols was the responsibility of J Division under Divisional Inspector Joseph Henry Helson. To co-ordinate and supervise these investigations, Swanson appointed Inspector First Class Frederick George Abberline. Inspectors Henry Moore and Walter Simon Andrews went with Abberline to the East End, who was familiar with the area having served as head of H Division CID prior to Reid. Abberline carried out his task conscientiously and with humanity, often giving prostitutes the money for their bed for the night.

Much criticism was to be levelled at the police during the hunt for the Ripper. *The New York Times* London correspondent described them as 'the stupidest Detectives in the World' and Queen Victoria also observed witheringly: 'The Queen fears that the Detective department is not as efficient as it might be.'

It is therefore worth repeating what Commissioner Warren told the *New York Herald* on 13 November 1888:

> We are following up slight clues all the time. We received about fourteen hundred letters. Every single idea was investigated … people talk as if nothing had been done … every slaughterhouse is under watch for a murderous Butcher. In fact every clue has been closely followed up, and there are some clues and ideas which still occupy our attention, but which it would be impolitic to foreshadow to the public.

Typical of the disappointments suffered by the police was the arrest of John Pizer on 10 September. The press was full of reports that the killer was a man of Jewish origin who wore a leather apron and was habitually violent towards prostitutes, and Pizer was said to be him. In fact he turned out to be innocent, as did a trio of other ostensibly promising suspects: William Pigott, Charles Ludwig and Jacob Isenschmid. They were all arrested in September and found to have no connection with the murders.

Dear Boss

The end of the month brought not only the double murder but also the infamous letter by which the Ripper christened himself.

25 September 1888

Dear Boss,

I keep on hearing the Police have caught me but they won't fix me just yet. I have laughed when they look so clever and talk about being on the right track. That joke about Leather Apron gave me real fits. I am down on whores and I shant quit ripping them until I do get buckled. Grand work the last job was. I gave the lady no time to squeal. How can they catch me now. I love my work and want to start again. You will soon hear of me and my funny little games. I saved some of the proper red stuff in a ginger beer bottle over the last job but it went thick like glue and I cant use it red ink is fit enough I hope ha ha. The next job I do I shall clip the ladies ears off and send it to the police officers just for jolly wouldn't you. Keep this letter back till I do a

*bit more work, then give it out straight. My knifes
so nice and sharp I want to get to work right away
if I get a chance. Good luck.*

yours truly

Jack the Ripper

*Don't mind me giving the trade name
Wasnt good enough to past this before I got all the red
ink off my hands curse it.
No luck yet. They say I'm a doctor now ha ha*

Although the police believed that the letter was a concoction, written by a journalist, the letter was photographed and facsimiles posted up on walls to see if anyone could identify the handwriting. Most modern-day researchers agree that the letter was a hoax despite the fact that Catherine Eddowes' right ear was cut obliquely through on the day after the letter was received by the police.

from Hell

Unhappily, publication of the letter led to the police being deluged with similar letters purporting to come from the killer. These included the following missive, received by George Lusk, Chair of the Whitechapel Vigilance Committee on 16 October:

From Hell.
Mr Lusk,

Sir

I send you half the kidne I took from one woman prasarved it for you tother piece I fried and ate it was very nise I may send you the bloody knif that took it out if you wate a whil longer.

Signed

Catch me when
you can
Mishter Lusk.

Accompanying the letter was half a human kidney matching that removed from Eddowes' body. Here again the consensus both then and now is that the letter and kidney were a hoax perpetrated by medical students, although Major Smith of the City police was a significant exception and believed the kidney to be genuine.

Crass Stupidity

The Eddowes murder had taken place on the City police's ground, bringing them into the case and immediately embroiling them in a controversy with their colleagues from the Met.

After leaving Mitre Square the murderer fled east back into the Met's territory. In Goulston Street he tossed a piece of Eddowes' bloodstained apron into the doorway of No. 108–19 where it was found at 2.55 a.m. on 30 September by Met PC Alfred Long.

Long also discovered the chalk message above the apron believed to read: 'The Juwes are the men That Will not be Blamed for nothing.'

Superintendent Thomas Arnold, the divisional commander of H Division, was summoned. After he consulted with Sir Charles Warren it was decided to expunge the words before it was light enough for them to be photographed, in case they led to an anti-Semitic riot. This was over the strident objections of City police Detective Constable Daniel Halse, who believed that a potentially valuable clue was being obliterated. Warren and Arnold's decision was also to be sharply criticised by Major Smith and Robert Anderson, describing the erasure as 'crass stupidity'. However, evidence was given at Eddowes' inquest of many similar messages scrawled up around the East End.

Anderson returned from holiday on 6 October and spent the next thirty-six hours reinvestigating the crimes. He discovered that in his absence, Abberline and his men had carried out house-to-house inquiries in a designated area running east to west from Great Garden Street to the City boundary and north to south from Buxton Street to the Whitechapel Road. The end product of this reinvestigation is summed up in Anderson's 1910 book *The Lighter Side of My Official Life*: 'the conclusion we came to was that he [the Ripper] and his people were certain low class Polish Jews.'

One suggestion was using bloodhounds to track the murderer when he struck again. Two were tried and found to be unsuitable for use in the streets. Unfortunately, stories were floated in the press that the dogs had gotten lost and even that they had bitten Commissioner Warren. Both stories were false but caused the police some embarrassment.

Resignation

The murder of Mary Jane Kelly on 9 November coincided with Warren's resignation. The commissioner had responded to press attacks on the police with an article in *Murray's Magazine*, only to be rebuked by the Home Office for publishing it without permission. Warren declined to accept such a limitation and sent in his resignation, which was accepted. His last act was to allow the offer of a pardon to be issued in his name for 'any accomplice not being a person who contrived or actually committed the murder who all give such information and evidence as shall lead to the discovery of the person or persons who committed the murder'.

Warren's resignation was announced in *The Times* on 13 November. The newspaper revealed Warren's deep-seated resentment about the way the Home Office had treated him in his dispute with James Monro, and Monro's subsequent resignation. It also described how the situation had worsened, with the Home Secretary seeking Monro's advice on matters relating to crime and the organisation of the detective staff. Warren complained that he had been saddled with all the responsibility whilst his freedom of action had been curtailed.

Warren was succeeded as commissioner by his nemesis, James Monro. With no further murders in December or the opening months of 1889, the hunt for the Ripper was scaled down. In March, Abberline was redeployed to other duties, leaving Inspector Moore to conduct any ongoing inquiries. The files on Jack the Ripper were closed in 1892.

The City police's Hunt

We know very little about the City police's hunt for the Ripper because the bulk of their files were destroyed during the Second World War. Their inquiries were led by Inspector James McWilliam, head of the Detective Department. According to Smith, he had men in plain clothes in the pubs of the East End keeping a watch for any likely suspects and he gave orders for couples to be followed after dark. The City does not seem to have shared information with their Met colleagues. The Home

Office requested a report about their inquiries but McWilliam's letter in response was so uninformative that a Home Office official annotated it: 'They evidently want to tell us nothing.'

But Henry Smith later went on record as disagreeing with Robert Anderson's view of the Ripper being a Polish Jew. In his memoirs *From Constable to Commissioner*, Smith attacked Anderson for anti-Semitism. He wrote that the Ripper 'completely beat me and every Police officer in London', but then added, 'I have no more idea now where he lived than I had twenty years ago'. The crime writer H.L. Adam nevertheless alleged that Smith claimed to know the killer's identity.

Sir Charles Warren left no views about who the Ripper was. James Monro, who was commissioner from 1888–90, told his son that that the Ripper should have been caught. Monro's theory has been described as 'a very hot potato' in a letter by his grandson, but we do not know what it was.

Chief Inspector John George Littlechild, lead detective of the controversial Department D, wrote to George Sims averring that 'a very likely suspect' was Francis Tumblety, an Irish-American Herbalist whom Littlechild termed as 'sycopathia [*sic*] sexualis' who harboured 'remarkable and bitter feelings' towards women. From this, Tumblety has been advanced as a suspect by modern-day researchers.

One man dismissed by Scotland Yard as the Ripper in February 1889 was William Henry Bury who was arrested in Dundee for the murder of his wife, a former East London prostitute. However, two Scotland Yard Detectives who travelled to Dundee for Bury's execution are said to have been rather more favourably impressed by his credentials as the Ripper.

Abberline retired in 1892 without formulating any view as to the killer's identity. But eleven years later he evidently became convinced that Severin Klosowski, aka George Chapman, a Polish barber-surgeon resident in the East End in 1888, was the Ripper. Klosowski was arrested by Detective Inspector George Godley – a detective sergeant in J Division in 1888 – for poisoning three women in South London and executed on 7 April 1903. *The Trial of George Chapman* also shows that Abberline allegedly telegraphed Godley: 'You have got Jack the Ripper at last.' Later he told the *Pall Mall Gazette*, published 24 March 1903: 'I cannot help feeling that this is the man we struggled so hard to capture 15 years ago.' As in Tumblety's case, some modern researchers believe Klosowski/Chapman to have been the murderer.

The most famous police document dealing with Jack the Ripper suspects was penned in February 1894 by Melville Macnaghten, the individual whose proposed appointment as assistant chief constable in 1888 had caused the final rift between Warren and Monro. Macnaghten was appointed to that position in 1889, becoming detective chief constable in 1890 after Williamson's death. He rose through the ranks, eventually retiring as assistant commissioner.

In 1894, Macnaghten was asked to prepare a report for the Home Office about a series of newspaper articles nominating one Thomas Hayne Cutbush as the Ripper. After dismissing Cutbush as a suspect, Macnaghten went on to delineate the cases against three men, 'anyone of whom would have been more likely than Cutbush to have committed this series of murders':

1) A Mr M.J. [Montague John] Druitt, said to be a doctor & of good family, who disappeared at the time of the Miller's Court murder, whose body [which was said to have been upwards of a month in the water] was found in the Thames on 31st December – or about seven weeks after that murder. He was sexually insane & from private info I have little doubt but that his own family believed him to have been the murderer.

2) Kosminski [Aaron Mordke)] a Polish Jew & resident in Whitechapel. This man became insane owing to many years indulgence in solitary vices. He had a great hatred of women, especially of the Prostitute class, & had strong homicidal tendencies; he was removed to a lunatic asylum about March, 1889. There were many circs connected with this man which made him a strong suspect.

3) Michael Ostrog a Russian doctor & a convict who was subsequently detained in a lunatic asylum as a homicidal maniac. This man's antecedents were of the worst possible type & his whereabouts at the time of the murders could never be ascertained.

In fact Ostrog is now known to have been in France during the Ripper crimes, and Macnaghten was in error in describing Druitt, his preferred suspect, as a doctor; he was a barrister (although his father was a surgeon).

But Aaron Kosminski was subsequently endorsed as a major Ripper suspect by Chief Inspector Swanson who implies that Kosminski was the 'low class Polish Jew' pinpointed by Robert Anderson. Anderson had written in *The Lighter Side of My Official Life* that the only person who ever had a good view of the Ripper had 'unhesitatingly' identified Anderson's suspect 'the instant he was confronted with him, but he refused to give evidence against him'.

Donald Swanson's personal copy of Anderson's book came to light in the 1980s. Under the words 'against him' Swanson had written in pencil:

> ... because the suspect was also a Jew and also because his evidence would convict the suspect, and witness would be the means of murderer being hanged which he did not wish to be left on his mind. DSS.

Swanson continued in the margin of the page, 'And after this identification which suspect knew, no other murder of this kind took place in London.'

Fleshing it out a little more, Swanson continued his jottings on the book's end papers:

> After the suspect had been identified at the seaside home [believed to refer to the police convalescent home in Brighton, opened in 1890] where he had been sent by us with difficulty in order to subject him to identification and he knew he was identified. On suspect's return to his brother's house in Whitechapel he was watched by police [City CID] by day and night. In a very short time the suspect with his hands tied behind his back he was taken to Stepney Workhouse and there to Colney Hatch and died shortly afterwards – Kosminski was the suspect – DSS

Swanson was wrong about Kosminski dying 'shortly afterwards'. He was in fact transferred from Colney Hatch Lunatic Asylum to the Leavesden Home where he passed away on 24 March 1919.

This has been a chapter dealing with failure, so it is fitting that we should close by noting that many of the techniques now used in hunting serial killers were pioneered by the Metropolitan Police in 1888, notably the command structure of the investigation, the use of outside experts such as Dr Bond and Dr Gabe (during the Kelly murder), the withholding of evidence to test confessions (at Kelly's inquest), the use of proactive techniques like distributing the enlargements of the Ripper letter, and, most important of all, the first criminal profile, prepared by Bond on 10 November 1888.

Bibliography

Adam, H.L. (ed.), *The Trial of George Chapman (Notable British Trials Series)* (London: Butterworth, 1930)

Evans, Stewart P. and Donald Rumbelow, *Jack the Ripper: Scotland Yard Investigates* (Stroud: The History Press, 2006)

Jones, Richard, 'The City of London Police', www.jack-the-ripper.org (2010)

Letter from Christopher Monro (grandson) to researcher/author Keith Skinner (14 November 1986)

Letter to journalist George R. Sims (23 September 1913)

Warren, Sir Charles, *Annual Report*, 31 December 1887

Pall Mall Gazette

8

The Press Had A Field Day!

Andrew O'Day

The nineteenth-century press

Kevin Williams has written about the shift from the press being dominated by the State, to offering religious and political freedom, to the emergence of the popular press in the nineteenth century – the time of Jack the Ripper. The press became popular as a result of social, economic and technological factors. New technology – notably the rotary press (1868) and the introduction of linotype (1876) – expanded the number of copies of papers that could be printed and their quality. There was also a growth in literacy; many people had more leisure time in which to read the papers; and, even more importantly, wages increased so that many people could afford to buy them. There was, furthermore, abolition on press taxes in the 1860s.

There had already been a popularisation of content. Williams reveals that papers like *The Times* were characterised by serious consideration of topical events. The duty of the journalist was to seek out the truth, often about sensitive government matters. However, this was contrasted by another form of journalism.

As Williams explains, while one would normally equate newspapers with factual reporting, in the 1800s the Sunday newspaper – the best-selling paper of the week – contained romance and crime fiction. This paved the way for the more radical press, known for containing serious political analysis, but also sensational reports on murders, robberies, and juicy scandals.

Rather uncomplimentary and amusing quotes reproduced by Williams come from Matthew Arnold, who labelled this journalism as 'feather-brained', and from Friedrich Nietzche, who stated that 'the rabble vomit their bile and call it a newspaper'.

Illustrated news

It was the nineteenth century, Williams adds, which also saw the appearance of illustrated newspapers on a much wider scale than before, made possible by other advances in print technology. These newspapers appealed to an illiterate and semi-literate audience. Precursors to publications such as *The Penny Illustrated Paper* (1861) and *The Illustrated Police News* (1864), which was not a journal for the police and reported extensively on the 'Ripper killings', were *The Illustrated London News* (1842) and *The Illustrated Weekly Times* (1843).

As Linda Stratmann notes, not only was *The Illustrated Police News* influenced by the penny dreadful novels but the late nineteenth century was 'the heyday of the murder trial as theatre'; crowds would gather outside the court to await the verdict to high-profile cases, while those inside the courtroom would scramble for the best seats or use opera glasses to see from the back. This is in addition to the crowds that had long gathered to see murder sites, ideas that can be seen in Ripper film and television productions and

1888 *Punch* cartoon 'Horrible London': 'There were men at murderous work in malodorous den, and the ghoul-women gruesomely staring. The whole sordid drama of murder and guilt, the steel that strikes home and the blood that is spilt, was pictured in realist colours …' (THP)

prefiguring Ripper walking tours. This prepared for the interest in crime in film and television broadly and enables us to see the appeal of *The Illustrated Police News* in context. While the paper can be seen as an example of so-called 'New Journalism' with its sensationalism, it also had an educational purpose.

1888 and the Autumn of Terror

As L. Perry Curtis notes, *The Times* was more modest in its reporting of the Whitechapel Murders than many of the papers which featured sensationalist headlines, wallowed in reporting the horrific details of the mutilations, and made allusions to Gothic literature, like the half-sane, half-insane title character of Robert Louis Stevenson's *The Strange Case of Dr Jekyll and Mr Hyde*. Culprits of such sensationalism included *The Star*, *The Daily Chronicle*, *The Daily Telegraph*, *The Evening News*, *The Globe*, *Lloyd's*, and *Reynolds*. Many of the daily and Sunday newspapers went out of their way to highlight the abysmal conditions of the East End as a 'foreign land', unlike regional papers such as the *East London Observer* and the *East London Advertiser*.

BLIND-MAN'S BUFF.
(As played by the Police.)
"TURN ROUND THREE TIMES,
AND CATCH WHOM YOU MAY!"

The famous cartoon from *Punch* of the police playing 'Blind-Man's Buff', 22 September 1888. (© THP)

Curtis also explores the papers' different angles to the murders: either the praiseworthiness or condemnation of the police's ability to enforce law and order, and whether the use of bloodhounds to detect the murderer was desirable. Radical papers, such as *Lloyd's*, also focused on the need for social reform in the East End, and reminded readers of Sir Charles Warren's shamefully quashing a worker's revolt in Trafalgar Square the previous year ('Bloody Sunday'). Some journals indeed critiqued the press' resort to sensationalist reporting of gruesome crimes and conditions experienced by real people. Papers included carefully selected 'Letters to the Editor', focusing on these, and other issues.

Looking at illustrations, *Punch* magazine was famous for featuring a number of cartoons, for example, of the police playing 'Blind-Man's Buff' (22 September 1888), and of the Ripper as a knife-wielding phantom (29 September 1888).

The Illustrated Police News

The Illustrated Police News was, as Stratmann has noted, known for blending fact and fiction: such as conveying the Ripper murders in a sensationalistic manner using conventions of fiction. In this way, it differed from, for example, *The Penny Illustrated Paper*, which featured Ripper covers, but in a less sensationalised way. For example, there was an image of a policeman shining his torch on to a corpse but with no sensational captions (8 September 1888), and the same for an image of Mary Jane Kelly admitting a man to her lodgings (17 December 1888).

The Illustrated Police News sensationalised the murders by attributing the deeds to an 'other', frequently using the words 'MONSTER' and 'FIEND' on its covers. The 15 September 1888 cover features a police officer 'MAKING INQUIRIES AT THE SLAUGHTER HOUSE' and a week later the 22 September edition presents drawings of

Annie Chapman before and after death, with two men and a horse at a slaughter yard pictured below. By 17 November 1888 we are told that a victim was 'PICKED OUT FOR SLAUGHTER BY THE EAST-END FIEND'. The letters signed 'Jack the Ripper' and the parcel supposedly containing Catherine Eddowes' kidney, felt by many to have been sent by journalists trying to sensationalise the murders, were the subject of covers, with the Ripper depicted as a cannibal who had eaten the other kidney. The 8 December 1888 cover, meanwhile, is of Mary Jane Kelly opening the door to her lodgings to admit the Grim Reaper menacingly leaning towards her.

Death through tight lacing

As Stratmann notes, this fits in with the way that *The Illustrated Police News* was driven by what would make a good illustration. Images of the Grim Reaper appeared on numerous covers such as one depicting 'DEATH THROUGH TIGHT LACING' (25 June 1870), one depicting 'THE COMPULSORY VACCINATION ACT' (3 July 1886), one where Death was lurching towards murderer Frederick Deeming with an arrow (14 May 1892), and one depicting 'THE PLAGUE OF 1892' where Death was portrayed as a winged figure. *The Illustrated Police News*'s concern with imaginative illustrations was highlighted on another Ripper cover, where the female allegorical figure of Justice stands blindfolded over one of the gorily murdered prostitutes with the murderer presented dashing through an archway, his face not seen.

The Illustrated Police News is a prime example of the way in which the press serialised the Jack the Ripper murders in order to engage the reader of the day in an ongoing narrative. Even before the canonical five Ripper murders, the paper was highlighting the killings of Emma Smith and Martha Tabram as part of this series. Headlines emphasised the 'LATEST' victims of 'MYSTERIOUS' crime (15 September 1888, 22 September 1888,

29 September 1888) and the sequence of murders such as
'THE SEVENTH HORRIBLE MURDER BY THE MONSTER OF
THE EAST-END' (17 November 1888). Additionally, questions
were posed such as 'TWO MORE WHITECHAPEL HORRORS.
WHEN WILL THE MURDERER BE CAPTURED?' (6 October 1888)
and 'EAST END HORRORS. WHEN WILL THEY CEASE?'
(8 December 1888).

Furthermore, *The Illustrated Police News* commonly used the
technique of storyboarding where narratives were presented in a
sequential cartoon-like form, which made it ideal for telling the
on-going Ripper narrative. An ongoing narrative is present, for

The Illustrated Police News front page highlighting the murder of Mary Jane
Kelly, 17 November 1888. (© *The Illustrated Police News*, 1888)

instance, on the cover of the 13 October 1888 edition with the headline: 'SKETCHES OF THE FIENDISH WORK OF THE MONSTER OF WHITECHAPEL. HIS SIX CRIMES.' Captions accompanying images read 'THE FIRST OF THE SERIES OF WHITECHAPEL HORRORS', 'TAKING THE DYING DEPOSITIONS OF THE FIRST VICTIM OF THE WHITECHAPEL MONSTER', 'THE WHITECHAPEL MONSTER VISITS HANBURY STREET, 'HOW THE MONSTER ESCAPES AFTER HIS FIENDISH WORK', 'THE MURDERER SEEN WITH HIS LATEST VICTIM' and 'THE MONSTER BUYING FRUIT FOR ONE OF HIS DUPES'. There are also snippets of dialogue such as a victim stating 'I SHARNT BE LONG GETTING MY BED MONEY LOOK AT MY SMART BONNET'.

The haunting: the press post, 1888

Not only did the press of the day seize upon the Gothic notion of Jack the Ripper as a Jekyll and Hyde, killing in dark secluded spots in the East End of London, but also on the Gothic idea of the past haunting the present. Jack the Ripper was not laid to rest but was continually resurrected.

With hindsight, the slaughter of Mary Jane Kelly in November 1888 is commonly viewed as the final Ripper murder, but at the time there was no reason for the public to believe that the spree of killings had ended. The Ripper was never captured or unmasked, meaning that the murders were not given closure. Further murders, therefore, enabled the papers to continue the Ripper story in a serialised and sensationalistic fashion.

As Curtis notes, *The Star*, for example, connected the murder of an unfortunate named 'Lizzie' with the Ripper (24 December 1888), while *The Pall Mall Gazette* had tied the attack of Annie Farmer with the previous murders (21 November 1888) before reporting that the Ripper had fled to New York (31 December 1888).

However, in 1889 the press reported that the Ripper had struck again in the East End and claimed the life of Alice McKenzie, probably, like the canonical Ripper victims, a prostitute. *The Illustrated Police News* featured a portrait of McKenzie with the caption alongside it reading 'BEFORE MEETING WITH THE WHITECHAPEL FIEND'.

The papers also speculated as to whether the Pinchin Street murder of 10 September 1889, where an unidentified woman had been decapitated, was the work of Jack the Ripper, though many have argued that it was the work of the Torso Killer. As Curtis states, the headline in *The Times* (11 September 1889) was not as sensational as that of, for instance, *The Pall Mall Gazette* (10 September 1889). *The Illustrated Police News* of 21 September 1889 ran the headline 'THE NINTH WHITECHAPEL MYSTERY: IS IT THE WORK OF JACK THE RIPPER?' engaging the reader in the continuing narrative. In the centre was the all-too-common image of a police constable shining his torch on the mutilated corpse, while on the left- and right-hand sides were images including the murderer (left), the investigators of the case, and the location where the body was found (right).

Prostitute Frances Coles, whose body was discovered in the early hours of 13 February 1891, some two and a bit years after the mutilation of Mary Jane Kelly, was also suggested as a possible victim of Jack the Ripper by the papers. As noted on the Casebook website, on 14 February 1891 *The Times* reported that, although the murder of Coles was 'not so fiendish in all its details' as the previous killings, 'The place, the time, the character of the victim, and other points of resemblance, recall in the most obvious way the series of crimes associated in the popular mind with the so-called "Jack the Ripper".' On the same day, *The East London Advertiser* positioned Coles' death within 'the series of terrible crimes' which had 'been connected with East London during late years'.

The Illustrated Police News continued the graphic narrative of its earlier editions, announcing in its headline 'THE LATEST MYSTERIOUS MURDER OF WHITECHAPEL' and under a centrally positioned illustration of Coles ran the caption 'FRANCIS COLES THE LATEST VICTIM OF JACK THE RIPPER'. In the same manner as the reporting of the other murders, surrounding this image on the left were drawings of Coles being propositioned by a mysterious man under an archway, while on the right again were illustrations of the police constable riding towards the location where the murder had taken place and then shining a torch on the corpse. In the centre foreground was an image of Coles lying in her coffin.

Therefore, these women are as important to the Ripper narrative as the canonical five.

Speculation

With the killer masked there was also further speculation in the press as to the Ripper's identity. *The Illustrated Police News*, for example, featured such cover about Dr Lyttleton Forbes Winslow, born in 1844, who used to cast himself as Jack the Ripper. The headline read 'DR. FORBES WINSLOW CONJURES UP THE SECRET ACTIONS OF JACK THE RIPPER'. In the centre there was an image of a man menacingly grabbing a woman by the waist, underneath which reads 'JACK THE RIPPER'S DARING ATTEMPT TO ADD ANOTHER VICTIM TO HIS FEARFUL RECORD'. To the left were images of him writing about loose women, carrying a sack containing his murderous tools, and entering a house. To the right top was an image of the Ripper observed washing the blood off his hands on the morning of a murder, while to the left bottom he silently approaches one of his victims.

Another example of a suspect, featured on the cover of 16 April 1892, was Frederick Bailey Deeming, noted earlier. Hanged on 23 May 1892 for the murder of his first and second wife and his four children (all of whom were discovered concealed under the floorboards of his house) he had told his fellow prison inmates that he was Jack the Ripper. According to him, he had been driven insane by a venereal disease he had contracted on a sea voyage.

Television representations of the press

The importance of the press' involvement in the Ripper murders has been highlighted in television productions. These visit themes of the sensationalist reporting of the murders in 1888 and the way in which the killings haunted the popular imagination post-1888.

Significant productions in which the nineteenth-century press features are:

Jack the Ripper (directed by David Wickes, Euston Films, 1988)
Ripper Street (BBC, 2012)

Jack the Ripper

The first of these productions, the 1988 mini-series marking the centennial of the Ripper murders, places the killings firmly in the context of the sensationalist journalism of the day. The mini-series opens with paper boys running through the streets crying 'Murder in Whitechapel, Get *The Star*' and later shouting 'Ripper Eats Kidney', with the words 'Cannibal Ripper' on a placard, in order to attract punters to buy the paper.

One of the characters is a cheeky young journalist for *The Star*, Benjamin Bates, stereotypical of the new type of journalist. He relishes in the fact that the killings are selling papers, and delights in the gossip that Prince Eddy has been frequenting Whitechapel brothels, to the extent that Abberline's second-in-command, Sergeant Godley, has to warn Bates that if he prints a word not only will the edition be seized but he will also be locked up, something which would give Godley great pleasure.

Bates also takes clairvoyant Robert James Lees to the theatre to see Richard Mansfield star in *Jekyll and Hyde* after Lees provides a description of the killer from his vision which resembles Mansfield playing Robert Louis Stevenson's mad scientist. He then teams up with George Lusk, encouraging a riot against Sir Charles Warren for his mishandling of the investigation, and an interesting comparison can be made between the cheeky young journalist and the revolutionary Lusk. Both are using the Ripper murders to further their goals: Lusk's in starting a riot and Bates' in selling papers.

Upon hearing the epithet 'Jack the Ripper' for the first time Bates enthuses that 'It's a newspaper man's dream' and later delights in showing the police the package supposedly containing victim Catherine Eddowes' kidney. While the police are disgusted at the sight of the kidney, with Godley throwing the box in which it is contained down in horror, Bates remarks to an associate, 'I bet he [the Ripper] ate it with sage and onion.'

Ripper Street

The more recent production, *Ripper Street*, is set post-1888. This makes it ideal for exploring, albeit briefly, the way in which the press resurrected the Ripper, his presence haunting the public imagination in a Gothic fashion. *Ripper Street* differed from previous Jack the Ripper productions since, rather than focusing on the Ripper murders, it was a drama series dealing with other fictional crimes of the day. However, the first episode, screened in 2012, concerned the fall-out from the Ripper killings.

This episode, 'I Need Light', begins with a guided Ripper walking tour which ends abruptly with participants running away screaming after stumbling across the mutilated corpse of a woman. In this episode, Fred Best (journalist for *The Star*) has altered a crime scene to make it look as though the Ripper is continuing his spree of murders. In an important scene he is confronted in his office by Inspector Reid.

The *mise en scène* is striking. Before Best enters the office, Reid stands by framed newspaper reports concerning the Ripper killings. When Best walks in, Reid forces his arms behind his back and makes him face different symbolic framed newspaper reports. In front of a picture of a policeman discovering a body, Reid asks Best how he thought the mutilated women felt and asks if he had a pity for the many men he'd ruined with his accusations – with a report on John Pizer on the wall. Reid also tells him that he'd printed a letter that Reid hadn't credited as bona fide – with a report on this letter on the wall.

Best reveals that he and Abberline think the Ripper is back and taunts the police for not capturing the murderer. Reid claims he will be back for some ripping of his own if Best prints a word and so Best gives him a time limit in which to prove that the latest killings are the work of another knifeman, which is done. The closing message is that the East End must move on from the haunting of Jack the Ripper.

Jack the Ripper's legacy

However, the press treatment of the Ripper murders has had a lasting impact in another way. Not only did the visual press' treatment of the murders prefigure the cinematic, and later television, presentation of the Ripper narrative, but also the late nineteenth-century newspapers can be seen as precursors of tabloidisation in the era of the media baron. Tabloidisation refers to both the size of newspapers and also to the sensationalist reporting in newspapers, some of which (like *The Daily Mail*, *The Daily Express* and *The Daily Mirror*) first appeared at the turn of the twentieth century. This was a time when, as Williams notes, Lord Northcliffe's famous motto was 'get me a murder a day'. Photographs, as opposed to drawings, usually grace the front covers with alliterative and sensationalist headlines designed to get people to buy the papers. While the rise of the Internet encourages democratic 'citizen journalism', with people writing online blogs and contributing to YouTube, and while popular newspapers can be read online, the print media still has a place in today's society.

Bibliography

Curtis, L. Perry, *Jack the Ripper and the London Press* (New Haven: Yale University Press, 2001)

Stratmann, Linda, *Cruel Deeds and Dreadful Calamities: The Illustrated Police News 1864–1938* (London: British Library, 2011)

Williams, Kevin, *Get Me a Murder a Day!: A History of Media and Communication in Britain* (London: Bloomsbury, 2010)

9

The East End Of 1888: What Was It Really Like?

Edward Stow

We are supposed to think of Jack the Ripper's East End hunting ground as being an urban cesspit, with squalor rubbing shoulders with depravity. The area is depicted as comprising the worst streets in London, where policemen feared to tread unless in twos, with drunkenness, criminality and destitution being the norm. A landscape punctuated by dosshouses, hovels and tenements with rubbish, raw sewage and smog assaulting the senses.

The Jack the Ripper murders certainly put the East End under the spotlight, and not just domestically. For example, just a year later, the *New York Sun* (8 December 1889) carried an account in which one of its intrepid reporters accompanied an 'Inspector Harris' (certainly a made-up name to protect the policeman, generally believed to be Inspector Reid) on perhaps one of the first Jack the Ripper tours to grace these mean streets.

This account contains the stereotypes that have since become the common currency when setting the scene for these crimes:

Emerging from the underground at the Aldgate station, we came out upon Whitechapel road. This broad thoroughfare runs from Aldgate High Street to Mile End, and cannot fail to remind a New Yorker of the Bowery. Like the Bowery, it is brilliantly lighted all night; likewise there is a saloon on every corner, and it is the pleasure ground of pickpockets, thieves, prostitutes, and criminals of all ages, degrees, and previous condition of penal servitude. Like the Bowery, too, it is a dirty channel between dirtier slums, and, like the Bowery, it is livelier by night than by day. At this hour both sidewalks and the pavement swarmed with passengers whose personnel included the lees of London with the dregs of two continents and two score nations. The majority of this great throng, of course, was English, but in it savage-faced Lascars and Malays in sailors' blouses; unkempt, swarthy Turks in native costume; ragged, picturesque and various fakirs of Cathay; Arabs with dirty red fezes about their greasy heads, and various other breeds of Asiatics mingled with the lowest order of Poles, Russians, Germans, Swedes, Italians, Spaniards, Alsatians, Frenchmen, and undoubtedly the human product of every parallel that circles this great globe. Men and women were thronging into the public houses; dirty children sported in the gutters; ruffianly boys played pranks upon each other and the passer by; and slatternly young girls, with depraved faces, strolled along the sidewalks in groups, exchanging coarse jests with the half-drunken men who gathered before the groggery doors ...

One of the most famous cartoons of them all, depicting the
horrors of East End poverty as a cloaked spectre with a knife:
the Nemesis of Neglect. (THP)

It only gets worse

Scarcely had we crossed the street after this episode when
another sidewalk gathering fell apart, and a girl, not more
than 16 or 17 years of age, lurched out of it and reeled
up against the wall of the nearest building, while a shout
of laughter went up from the men and women about her.
She was so drunk that she could scarcely move or speak;
and as she staggered along, groping blindly against the wall,
the pedestrians turned laughingly away. The policemen, who
were scattered thickly along the sidewalk, paid no attention to
her, and the friend, who was used to such spectacles, informed
us that if they took every drunken woman into custody they
found in Whitechapel on a Saturday night they would find
little time to do anything else.

It is something that impresses all Americans in London –
the number of drunken women one sees in the streets.
The condition is probably due to the circumstance that
women stand up and drink at all the London bars with the
same freedom as the men. Indeed, on almost any afternoon or
evening in any of the lower-class bars – and there are scarcely
any high-class ones, except the hotels, the theatres, and the
swellest restaurants – one will find as many women as men
gathered before the counter. One sees, even in Pall Mall and
Piccadilly in mid-afternoon, drunken women who stagger
along unmolested by the policemen. We saw more drunken
women than drunken men during our tour that night in
Whitechapel.

Old folk

'Inspector Harris' continued his tour:

> No more pitiful spectacle can be imagined than these wretched animal wrecks, beings that once were human now sunken lower than the vilest beasts, the divine imprint long since seared from mind and soul. Gray hair that in other circumstances might have been venerable, but now more dishonored and dishonorable than in sinful youth, straggling from under tattered bonnets, or oftener uncovered to the November winds; bodies rent and sore with the most fearful maladies; faces utterly bereft of human expression, toothless mouths, and eyes bleared and glazed; scant and bedraggled, vermin-infested clothing that scarce holds together; bare feet, or boots broken and showing lack of stockings, as torn shirts betray the lack of underclothing! The picture is not overdrawn.

Not overdrawn? The article continued in similar vein for four long columns!

Wilton's music hall

Responsible for much of the drunkenness was Charrington's Brewery, then on Mile End Road – or at least Frederick Charrington, the heir to this industrial empire, certainly felt so. In 1870, at the age of 20, he set up the evangelical Tower Hamlets Mission, which is still on Mile End Road, although the brewery is now a trading estate! Frederick Charrington's life story is recounted in *The Great Acceptance* by Guy Thorne (1913).

Here is another taste of the East End, this time describing a venue that still stands (but with a different clientele):

Wilton's Music Hall, or, as it was affectionately called by its habitués, 'The Mahogany Bar', was a music hall opening on a quiet square notorious as the Ratcliffe Highway, then regarded as the most disreputable street of its kind in the whole world. Ratcliffe Highway … was the resort of the lowest characters of all nations, the very scum of the earth. It was here that 'Poor Jack' fell a prey to the vilest harpies in Christendom, it was a den of prostitution, vice, drunkenness and crime, tenanted by fiends in human form, who made their unholy gains out of the passionate outbursts of the misguided sailors, who, by their orgies, their desperate affrays, and frightful excesses, did so much to confer its evil notoriety upon the street.

Incidentally that was not 'Poor Jack the Ripper'! It was 'Poor Jolly Jack Tar', the sailor on shore leave from the nearby docks. If the late Victorian Wilton's was bad, what of the rest of the East End? Does Guy Thorn confirm the American reporter's estimation?

The collection of little villages which clustered round that great stronghold of the English kings, the Tower, had been swept away so utterly that no single trace remained. But the name still existed, and that Sahara of crowded, pestilential dwellings, of narrow streets, where vice and famine walked hand in hand, that unknown city of the lost, still retained the pleasant title of the 'Tower Hamlets', with all its associations of village greens, sweet trees, and simple homesteads.

But surely the other music halls were not as bad as Wilton's?

Lusby's music hall was, without doubt, a sink of iniquity. It was notorious in the locality, but it also spread its evil tentacles westwards. The well-to-do, foolish, and drunken young 'bloods' of the period – I believe 'masher' was their designation at the time – used to drive down in cabs from Piccadilly and haunt Lusby's in pursuit of the girls of the East End. It was a new sensation. It provided an evening's amusement quite out of the common.

The East End was a tourist attraction for West-End gentry keen to rough it for the night!

Deprivation

The American author Jack London's *People of the Abyss* is frequently quoted to illustrate East End deprivation at the time of Jack the Ripper. However, he wrote in 1902, many years after the events and he was writing for a purpose. A taste of Jack London's polemics can be gleaned from his first venture out east to Stepney station:

> … the region my hansom was now penetrating was one unending slum. The streets were filled with a new and different race of people, short of stature, and wretched or beer-sodden appearance. We rolled along through miles of bricks and squalor, and from each cross street and alley flashed long vistas of bricks and misery. Here and there lurched a drunken man or woman, and the air was obscene with sounds of jangling and squabbling. At a market, tottery old men and women were searching in the garbage thrown in the mud for rotten potatoes, beans and vegetables …

Stepney Station is now named Limehouse and is on the dockland's light railway. To get there, Jack London's cab must have taken him down Commercial Road. This is a wide thoroughfare and contemporary photographs do not show it in the same light.

The East End was an easy antithesis for the West End. They were polar opposites: the rich and the poor; the rulers and the downtrodden. But the East End had its draws: the docks, the markets, the music halls. It made for an interesting canvas. It wouldn't have been so 'neat' had the Jack the Ripper murders happened 'over the river' on the south bank or perhaps in the drab slums of North London around Finsbury and the Caledonian Road. The polemic writings of journalists and authors keen for a readership with exotic tales of East End degradation should not perhaps be taken completely at face value. Are any other sources available to us when appraising the East End of this period?

Council housing

The first council housing built in Britain was constructed in the East End, but not in the area associated with Jack the Ripper. It was the boundary estate which stands to this day in the north-west quarter of Bethnal Green. It was built in 1900 over a district known as the Old Nichol, which some writers characterised as being the worst in the area and a breeding ground of gangs. Later mythology suggested the 'Old Nichol Gang' may have been responsible for some of the earlier Whitechapel Murders that are not usually attributed to Jack the Ripper. Nevertheless, it is interesting that the Old Nichol was chosen for the first systematic and extensive slum clearance with it being replaced by improved public-sector council housing.

William Booth

The Salvation Army was founded by William Booth in 1865 as the East London Christian Mission. The docks gave the East End a polyglot character as it had more migrants than any other area of London; there were growing numbers of Jewish refugees and the docks attracted a large number of Irish workers. There were souls to save and convert, and undoubtedly there were a lot of poor people in need of succour. Booth's first outings as an open-air preacher had been in the less-fashionably poor South Bank. When he pitched up on Mile End Waste, just yards from where Charrington was to open his mission a few years later, Booth was in effect headhunted by an existing group of organised missionaries. It could be argued that Booth established the Salvation Army in the East End because it was more socially organised than the poorer South Bank.

Degrees of poverty

We know the South Bank was poorer because William Booth's namesake, the unrelated Charles Booth, conducted a monumental survey, the results of which were published from 1889 onwards as the *Life and Labour of the People in London*. Booth (Charles, there is always a danger of confusion with these Booths) produced a series of maps to illustrate the degrees of poverty with each street shaded a different colour. Black meant the lowest class – vicious and semi-criminal. Dark blue was slightly better – very poor. The colours got lighter as the residents grew in prosperity. Red was middle class and yellowy gold (appropriately) for the upper-class districts.

The Old Nichol is dark blue and black and Dorset Street in Whitechapel is also black. Dorset Street was, in fact, often termed the worst street in London. It was here that the last canonical Jack the Ripper victim, Mary Kelly, lived and died. Annie Chapman also lived on Dorset Street.

Booth also produced another map ('Map Shewing Degrees of Poverty in London 1889–1890') in which he divided London up into 134 districts each of roughly 30,000 inhabitants. Based on the information he had obtained from his street survey, Booth then determined the percentage degree of poverty in each district. Booth's definition of poverty was a household earning less than 21s a week (roughly £95 in today's terms).

Of the ten poorest districts, five lined the South Bank of the Thames, two were in North London (around Caledonian Road and Finsbury) and three were in the East End; but the East End districts were not associated with the Jack the Ripper murders. They were the western part of Bethnal Green (i.e. the Old Nichol), an area around Bromley-by-Bow (part of Poplar) and the Wapping docks.

Overcrowding

Booth also calculated the population density. This told a different tale. Of the top ten districts for overcrowding, three are intimately associated with the Ripper murders (Whitechapel and the areas to the immediate east of the City of London). This is perhaps surprising as the culprit could choose his killing ground. Apart from Mary Kelly, the killings took place in the open and in the most crowded part of London. Yet the killer remained at large; perhaps he had reason to choose those streets.

The Booth district that included Dorset Street – the murder scenes of Mary Kelly, and the non-canonical Frances Coles and Alice Mackenzie, and where Catherine Eddowes' bloody apron was found under a chalked message in Goulston Street – was the eighth most overcrowded in London. It squeezed in 256 people per acre, but was only 58th out of 134 in terms of degree of poverty.

Labour

An examination of the political hue of the East End tends to validate the statistics gathered by Charles Booth. The standard reference for this area of study is *Behind the Lines: East London Labour 1914–1919* by Julia Bush.

The performance of the then-new rising force of Labour is likely to give an indication of the relative prosperity of different constituencies. It is undoubtedly the case that political organisation reflects the make-up of communities. Despite the great increase in male suffrage as the nineteenth century progressed to the twentieth and the steady growth of organised Trade Union power in the East End docks and factories, initially Labour support was confined to the poorest areas as identified by Charles Booth. Yet these were not areas associated with the Jack the Ripper murders.

In the London County Council elections held between 1889 and 1913, Labour only ever won seats in Bethnal Green North East, Bow and Bromley, Poplar and briefly in St George's in the East (which included Wapping).

The Metropolitan Borough of Stepney was created in 1900. All of Jack the Ripper's victims lived here and most of the Whitechapel Murders took place within its borders. Stepney briefly had one Labour councillor in 1903 out of sixty in total, but did not have any significant Labour representation until 1919 when Labour actually took control of the council. The only East End borough to regularly elect Labour councillors prior to 1919 was Poplar. By contrast in West Ham, then the outer East End and still part of Essex, Labour became the largest party as early as 1898. Yet by 1925 Labour had clear majorities in all the East End boroughs.

There were eight Parliamentary general elections between 1885 and 1910 and the same pattern emerges. Labour were only able to win seats in Bethnal Green North East and Bow and Bromley (part of Poplar). In the 1923 general election Labour won all but one of the East End seats.

Even when allowance is made for the organisational problems that undoubtedly inhibited the uniform growth of the new Labour Party, it is noticeable that the only parts of the East End where Labour were able to gain any sort of regular political representation were in the borough of Poplar and the north-east division of Bethnal Green. Yet soon after the First World War all of the East End was firm Labour territory.

The other areas of London that Booth identified as being particularly poor also had stronger Labour representation before the First World War than the Ripper streets of the East End. South of the river, this included Deptford, Woolwich and Lambeth.

The strong correlation between early Labour political representation and the poorest districts of London as identified by Booth's survey should not be very surprising. Perhaps the only surprising aspect is that the Ripper streets – the districts that were and are portrayed as being the very worst in London – were actually anything but that!

That does not imply that they were havens of middle-class respectability. All things are relative. Yet it is extremely misleading to picture these streets as being uniformly bad; it was a very mixed area, with comparative affluence rubbing shoulders with poverty.

The board

A perusal of the minute books of the Whitechapel District Board of Works for 1888 (held at Tower Hamlets Local History Library) is illuminating. Every detail was covered.

At a board meeting held on 13 August 1888, just before the Autumn of Terror commenced, they discussed how to improve the inadequate street lighting in a number of locations. This was to have some later significance as the lighting conditions were deemed partly responsible for the murders. At the same meeting, the finance committee submitted a report that explained that cheques totalling over £1,300 were required to pay for paving various streets. The Commercial Gas Company was paid over £1,000 for a quarter's street lighting and £5 5s was required for shovels for the removal of dust. They had to pay much more for the cartage of dust to their 'destructor', maintain the sewers and unblock traps. Overall expenditure came to over £5,590 18s 7d.

At this meeting the board also set up a special sanitary committee. Particular attention was paid to what were termed 'nuisances injurious to health' and action taken to eliminate such risks.

Typical local government functions that are recognisable today were also diligently undertaken. They had to regulate planning matters. A pub called the Blue Coat Boy on Norton Folgate requested a cellar opening stretching 4ft from their boundary. They were allowed 3ft!

A lamplighter named Smith was also reportedly taking action against the board for an accident he suffered in the course of his work. He sought £1,000 in damages, a small fortune, and the board resisted the claim.

The Ordnance Survey map

A glance at an old Ordnance Survey map of the East End from the 1893 will show public buildings, new railways, wash houses and tramways. We are not talking about a neglected slum. There were numerous music halls, which may have been unpopular with the temperance people but would not have prospered had the local residents not had a reasonable amount of disposable income.

The local boards of work were responsible for producing annual reports into sanitary conditions. The report of the Medical Officer for Health for Whitechapel District in 1893 recorded some interesting information: for example, the death rate for children under 5 was 26.3 per cent for London as a whole and 26 per cent for Whitechapel. These are staggeringly high figures but Whitechapel was slightly below the London average. For other forms of death that one might associate with deprived areas, the London-wide mortality rate for alcoholism was 0.75 per cent, but in Whitechapel only 0.15 per cent. Interestingly, for a study on serial killing, the violent death rate (homicide, suicide and execution) for London was 0.55 per cent, but in Whitechapel 0.36 per cent – it was, however, higher in 1888! There were two cases of manslaughter in Whitechapel in 1893 but no murders.

According to the 1891 census, around 57 per cent of the East End Eastern European Jewish refugees lived in Whitechapel District. Furthermore, no fewer than ninety-eight common lodging houses were registered in Whitechapel. This was the highest concentration in London. The biggest cluster was in Dorset Street, where there were fourteen.

It was the settlement of thousands of Jewish refugees fleeing from an unstable situation in Russia into overcrowded accommodation, together with the concentration of lodging houses in Whitechapel, that gave the area its high population density and contributed to the degree of poverty found by Booth.

Not a heavenly quarter, nor a cesspit

However, Booth found affluence alongside the poverty. This explains the otherwise strange phenomenon that is visible today. The surviving Victorian buildings that line the main East End thoroughfares, be they originally pubs, banks, public buildings, shops, or even early social housing, are invariably incredibly ornate. The windows, doorframes, and brickwork are designed for show. These are not simple buildings thrown up to satisfy the dregs of society.

It seems likely that the adverse publicity that the East End attracted as a result of the Ripper murders contributed to the flight of the remaining middle class and upper working class from the area and helped to solidify the East End as a homogenous working-class district by the time of the First World War. It is telling that when Charles Dickens, who wrote and died before the Ripper murders took place, chose to describe poverty in London and slum living, he did not focus his descriptive powers on the East End. For example, *Oliver Twist* was set in the slums immediately to the north of the City of London.

So while the East End was not a heavenly quarter, neither was it a total cesspit. In 1888 it was far from being the most deprived area of London and considerable expense and effort were expended to continuously improve the area. It suited contemporary writers to dwell on the downside as this fitted with the overall narrative; the semi-destitute prostitutes from the poorest areas of the East End were, after all, the victims. Just as the Ripper murders became part of the East End folk culture, they also became an integral part of how the East End was identified by the rest of the world. Inevitably this reinforced the status of the East End as a working-class or even sub-working-class ghetto, which became a self-fulfilling prophecy in the early twentieth century.

10

If The Hat Fits:
The Suspects: Part One

David Bullock

At 3.45 a.m. on 31 August 1888, Mary Nichols drew her final breath and a tragic life came to an unexpected end. Unbeknownst at the time, the Nichols murder was to be the opening chapter of a story that would grip the nation and has endured for 126 years: forming a tale of murder and madness bound within a mystery as intriguing as any in the history of crime.

Since the time of the Whitechapel Murders, when a lone figure struck fear into the heart of a country, the search for his identity has continued on. Today, over a hundred names are listed as potential suspects; from actors and artists to princes and their tutors, to those ordinary men who slipped under the radar of suspicion for too long; their names over time have become etched into our consciousness.

While many would ultimately be exonerated there are some individuals, named at the time of the killings and since, against whom the evidence continues to mount.

What follows are the stories of some of the first suspects to emerge after the murder of Mary Nichols, as a populace awoke to the reality of their plight and saw that within their labyrinthine world a new breed of killer was at work.

Pizer

At 8 a.m. on 10 September 1888, in the wake of the Ripper's second murder, a bootmaker by the name of John Pizer was sitting in a house in Mulberry Street – panicking. For several days the 38-year-old Pizer had refrained from leaving the property at the request of his brother, who had become concerned for his safety.

Since the start of the Ripper murders, rumours had circulated the district that the killer was known to be a local brute who had terrorised the prostitutes of the area: blackmailing most and beating others. The suspect was described as a stocky man of sinister expression and was known only by his nickname of 'Leather Apron', adopted due to his choice of clothing.

By 4 September the police were aware of the rumours and, keen to jump upon what was perceived as the first positive lead, began scouring the East End in search of the suspect. Conscious of the growing interest in the murder case, the press began following the hunt while exaggerating much of Leather Apron's character.

As London became enthralled in the search for a prime suspect, John Pizer, who was known to have used the nickname and worn a leather apron, began to fear the worst. As did his brother. The theory proved correct on 10 September when Sergeant William Thick knocked upon their front door.

Thick was an experienced officer who had honed his craft after twenty years of working within the Metropolitan Police. His fine knowledge of the East End and its inhabitants was second to none and thus, when Thick became aware of the gossip flittering throughout the dosshouses and taverns in the district, he realised that the suspect was in fact known to him.

Thick had been aware of John Pizer for some eighteen years. He knew his trade, his local haunts and, importantly, his nickname. After locating Pizer in Mulberry Street, Thick escorted the suspect to Leman Street Police Station. During the interview that followed, the bootmaker would confirm that he did indeed wear a leather apron but refused to accept that he was known by such a nickname.

Though at first Pizer appeared desperate, denying facts that were known to be true, he confidently proved he was in Holloway on the night of the Nichols murder. As a result, Sergeant Thick and his colleagues had no choice other than to re-evaluate their original thoughts.

Five hours before the Nichols murder, a fire had broken out in Shadwell Dry Docks which was so fierce it turned the dark skies red. Smoke and flames blistered the air and caught the interest of many of the locals, including John Pizer. According to his statement he had stood on the Holloway Road and watched the fire, during which time he had briefly spoken to a constable. Then he took a bed in a local lodging house.

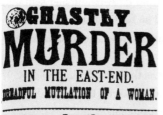

Pizer's account was soon verified and though he would be required to take part in an identity parade, it became quickly apparent that he was in no way connected to the Ripper murders. Although cleared of any connection to the murder case, for Pizer the worst was yet to come. As a consequence of the press coverage surrounding his arrest, he was still seen as a threat to the people of Whitechapel.

The suspect 'Leather Apron' was captured by Sergeant William Thick.
(© Casebook.org)

After his release from custody on 11 September, walking the streets became an obstacle course of taunts and physical assault. Pizer would eventually seek and successfully receive compensation from those newspapers who had portrayed him as a murderer.

Isenschmid

On the very day that saw John Pizer released from custody, two doctors – named Crabb and Cowan – attended Holloway Police Station wishing to express their concerns about a suspicious lodger residing at No. 60 Mitford Road. The man's name was Jacob Isenschmid and, according to the two men, he had been living at the property for six days.

In light of the John Pizer affair, which had seen a key suspect exonerated, the police were quick to act. They visited the named premises and spoke to the landlord, where it was confirmed that Isenschmid had recently parted from his wife and had kept odd hours since occupying the room. The landlord also added that on the morning of the Annie Chapman murder, Isenschmid had not been present at the house.

Detective Inspector Styles was then dispatched to No. 97 Duncombe Road to locate and speak to Isenschmid's wife. This interview would prove most enlightening.

Mary Isenschmid confirmed that she hadn't seen her husband for two months. She gave his profession as a butcher and confirmed that he often carried large knives that he used in his trade. Mary also stated that approximately six years earlier her husband had suffered a fit. Since then he had began to lose his grip on reality, adding that he was prone to violent outbursts.

Fortunately for Styles, Isenschmid was not a difficult man to find. By 12 September he had been arrested and removed to Holloway Police Station. Though the police were satisfied with their arrest, it became apparent almost immediately that Jacob Isenschmid was mentally unstable. He was subsequently removed to a workhouse and soon after admitted into a psychiatric unit.

It would later transpire that Isenschmid's mental health had been in steady decline for around a year and that he had been a patient at Colney Hatch Asylum. After his release, though he had appeared cured, his mind soon became unhinged. He abandoned his wife and fled from his employers, surviving on the money he made from restaurants, selling sheep's heads and body parts that he bought from market.

After his arrest, police interest in Isenschmid as a suspect continued and grew stronger when new information was received from a key witness. Mrs Fiddymont claimed that at around 7 a.m. on 8 September, whilst at work in The Prince Albert pub, she had observed a man acting strangely.

Fiddymont recalled that as the man stepped inside the pub, she noticed his hands were stained with blood and observed that his eyes appeared wild. She confirmed that the male ordered a drink and then left. Mrs Chappel, a friend of Fiddymont's, also spotted the man and decided to follow him. Chappel had watched as the man walked nervously up the street but, scared to go any further, pointed him out to a passer-by who continued to follow as far as Bishopsgate.

When news of the Annie Chapman murder reached Fiddymont, she became suspicious. Hanbury Street was only a short distance from her pub at Brushfield Street and, given the timing of the discovery of Chapman's body, the subsequent sighting of the strange male suddenly appeared all the more important.

Fiddymont went on to describe the male as being around 40 years of age, with blonde hair and a ginger moustache. She recalled that he was wearing a black coat buttoned high to his neck and that his brown hat had been pulled low over his face. Isenschmid matched the description.

❦

Interest grew in Isenschmid's candidacy and by 19 September, Police Commissioner Sir Charles Warren stated that he was one of three men under suspicion of committing the murders.

It seemed the next logical step was for the police to verify whether Isenschmid was indeed the man described by Fiddymont. An attempt was made to conduct an identity parade. However, Isenschmid's doctor declined the notion, based on his patient being too ill to take part.

For a time it seemed that Isenschmid was a strong suspect. It was even discovered that he had previously made claims of being Leather Apron and thus directly implicated himself with the Whitechapel Murders. But on 30 September, Jack the Ripper struck again. He murdered two victims in a single morning, exonerating Jacob Isenschmid who at the time was still residing in Grove Hall Asylum.

Though he had seemed a promising suspect and might well have been the man observed by Mrs Fiddymont, Isenschmid could not have been Jack the Ripper.

Jacob Isenschmid would live for another twenty-two years, dying in 1910 while a patient of Colney Hatch Asylum.

Puckridge

On 4 August 1888, a 50-year-old chemist by the name of Oswald Puckridge was released from an asylum in London. He would leave the institution as cured and, once back amid the teeming streets of the capital, seemingly disappeared.

It would later be alleged that Puckridge had been educated as a surgeon. That he had in his possession a number of long bladed knives and that prior to the September of 1888 and owing to a deterioration of the mind, he had made threats to rip people up.

His release date came a month prior to the murder of Mary Nichols and only three days before the slaying of another prostitute named Martha Tabram, who some theorists believe was an early victim of the Ripper.

By September 1888, in the wake of three murders, the police had begun to see Puckridge as a likely suspect. In the report written by Sir Charles Warren, the commissioner confirmed that Puckridge was indeed under investigation. It also states that searches for him were being conducted; yet at the time of writing his whereabouts were still unknown.

Five years later, Puckridge was found on Queen Victoria Street close to the Thames. He would be admitted into Bow Infirmary and after only a short stay was discharged. Within three years Puckridge's mind gave way entirely, and he was admitted to the City of London Asylum.

By the spring of 1900, aged 61, Oswald Puckridge was dying. Now residing in Holborn Workhouse, he suffered ill health and died of bronchial pneumonia within a few days of his admittance.

Although on paper Puckridge appears a suspect worthy of closer examination, in 1888 he was 50, making him too old in comparison to witness descriptions of the Ripper that generally place the suspect as between 20 or 30 years of age.

There is also little evidence to support the claim that he had trained as a surgeon or had a history of violence. Therefore, without the benefit of further evidence, Puckridge's candidacy as the Ripper, though intriguing, must be looked upon with some caution.

Burrows

As the murders continued through the autumn and winter of 1888, the police became desperate. Arrests were constant, yet all too soon the would-be suspects were set free due to a lack of evidence. Working blind and without the benefit of forensics or criminal profiling, the police cast the net of suspicion wide, hoping to find the killer among a host of men labelled as potential suspects.

Such a tactic would inevitably throw up false leads and provide a haul of candidates who, in truth, were no more likely to have been the Ripper than the police officers who hunted him.

Due to the witness testimony of Israel Schwartz, who claimed to have seen the Ripper's third victim in company with a man wearing a peaked cap, on 8 December a vagrant by the name of Edwin Burrows was arrested simply due to the hat resting upon his head.

Burrows would prove to be innocent of any connection with the Ripper murders, yet his arrest exemplifies the sheer desperation felt by the police, who believed that no man was above suspicion.

Similar stories exist of other men who, like Burrows, were questioned and in one case arrested on multiple occasions due solely to having an appearance that was considered to be odd. And while the arrests were deemed necessary, with the police working on little evidence, the Ripper remained free.

Druitt

At 1 p.m. on the last day of 1888, a waterman by the name of Henry Winslade discovered the decaying remains of a male floating in the Thames, near Chiswick. The body was dragged from the water and within two days was identified as Montague John Druitt, a 31-year-old barrister and assistant schoolmaster.

William Druitt, the brother of the deceased, was present at the inquest and gave evidence, stating that weeks earlier he had become worried that his brother had disappeared. William had travelled to London and searched, but had been unable to locate him. When a suicide note was found at Montague's home, the truth of his disappearance was finally learnt.

In life, Montague Druitt had been well liked – an intelligent, articulate young man with a promising career ahead of him. In the latter months of 1888, however, things changed. His world began to crumble as he feared he was suffering from the same hereditary condition that had led his mother to an asylum several months earlier.

Unable to cope, at the beginning of December Druitt wrote a short note to his brother William. He left his lodgings, filled his pockets with stones and leapt into the cold waters of the Thames, remaining undiscovered for almost four weeks.

In truth the sad story of Montague John Druitt should have ended there, yet in 1894 his tale was resurrected in a report written by Chief Constable Melville Macnaghten.

In a confidential document, Macnaghten wrote of three men who he deemed likely to have been the Ripper and named Druitt as his preferred suspect. Macnaghten's belief, and one shared by many, was that the Ripper's last killing was that of Mary Kelly on 9 November 1888. December had passed without a murder and it was presumed that the spree was finally over.

One theory was that the culprit might have been imprisoned for some unrelated offence or had fled the country. Another opinion was that after murdering for the fifth time, the Ripper had taken his own life. Macnaghten considered this the most logical conclusion.

The chief constable wrote that Druitt was a doctor; he was 'sexually insane' and had disappeared at the time of the Kelly murder, and also that his own family believed he was the Ripper.

Should all the facts given by Macnaghten have been correct then Druitt would have indeed proved a plausible suspect, yet history tells us that many of the details provided by Macnaghten were incorrect. Druitt was not a doctor and rather than disappearing after the murder of Mary Kelly, he continued working until the end of November. As for the mention of a family's suspicion, no corroborating evidence was ever given to support such a claim. There is also no evidence of a violent nature or criminal past that would lead one to suspect Druitt of being capable of murder.

Druitt was a white male. He was tall and slim and of respectable appearance, which matches a number of eyewitness descriptions of the Ripper, but that is where any possible connection ends.

Unlike many suspects who at least were in the East End at the time of the murders, in one case Druitt was as far afield as Dorset at the time of the killings. Due, however, to Macnaghten's conviction, Druitt will forever remain a viable candidate and even today is hailed by some as the most likely.

Sadler

In February 1891, 53-year-old James Thomas Sadler arrived back in Whitechapel after working at sea. Though, as a ship's fireman, Sadler travelled extensively, he was perhaps never happier than when back in the familiar surroundings of London's East End.

On 11 February, Sadler was discharged from his ship and, armed with his wages, sought out the company of local prostitute Frances Coles. For almost two days the pair were inseparable until the morning of 13 February, when tragedy struck.

At 2.15 a.m. Coles was found dead, murdered in a grim alleyway known as Swallow Gardens. Her body was found by Constable Ernest Thompson who claimed to have heard footsteps fleeing the area shortly before discovering the body. It would later be learnt that Coles had been violently thrown to the ground after which her attacker had slit her throat.

Due to her murder being so reminiscent of the Ripper's crimes, in both its location and method, all too soon whispers began to circulate the district that the Whitechapel monster was back. But, unlike the Ripper case, on this occasion the police had only one suspect in mind. Sadler was known to be violent and due to the fact that he had been in company with Coles prior to the murder, was seen in the vicinity of Swallow Gardens and was found to have had a knife in his possession at the time, on 15 February he was arrested.

The story naturally made the headlines. If Coles was a Ripper victim and Sadler her killer, then it was logical to believe that finally the Ripper had been caught. But as strong as the case against Sadler may have appeared soon, aided by solicitors, the truth began to emerge.

Sadler's knife was deemed too blunt to have inflicted the wounds. Witnesses confirmed that Sadler had not been in company with Coles in the hours preceding her death and Sergeant Wesley Edwards was able to confirm that at 2 a.m. Sadler had been spotted outside the royal mint, at which time he appeared drunk and was struggling to walk. He also had alibis for the times of the previous Ripper murders. By 2 March the charges were dropped.

The police appear to have been displeased with this decision as Sadler remained under observation. The existing evidence indicates that Sadler was indeed a brute who regularly beat his wife and instilled fear in those who knew him. To this day, though absolved of any connection to the Coles murder, to some he remains the only plausible suspect.

11

Have You Seen The Devil?
The Suspects: Part Two

David Bullock

Today, thanks to a host of historians and researchers, we know more about the crimes of Jack the Ripper than ever before. Over a century since the time of killings and aided by newly discovered evidence, we can now look upon the investigation with fresh eyes and in doing so uncover new and credible suspects.

Due to the number of serial killers who followed in the Ripper's footsteps, we can now profile the type of individual who commits multiple murders: in most cases the killers are male, aged in their 20s or 30s, from dysfunctional families and generally will take menial jobs. Their victims are often strangers and usually they are adept at hiding their true character behind a mask of normality.

Armed with such a profile and a wealth of witness testimony from those who claimed to have seen the Ripper, we can analyse the case with renewed vigour, mindful that any viable suspect must meet certain criteria.

The man we seek must have the capability and motive to commit murder; he must resemble the appearance of the killer and must be able to answer the biggest mystery of the entire saga – why did the Ripper stop?

While it would be virtually impossible to explore every suspect proposed since the publication of Tom Cullen's *Autumn of Terror* in 1965, through careful study we are able to discover the existence of a small pool of suspects who exhibit elements of the psychological and physical profile of Jack the Ripper, demonstrating both the capacity to kill as well as the cunning required to escape detection.

Kelly

There are many theorists who believe that the perpetrator of the Whitechapel Murders was a lunatic; either a former patient of an asylum released at the time of the murders or an escapee on the run during 1888.

Though many examples exist of patients who were at large at the time of the killings, of them all the case against James Kelly is perhaps the most convincing.

On 21 June 1883, Kelly attacked his wife, Sarah, stabbing her in the throat at their home in Cottage Lane, London. Three days later Sarah died from her injuries. Kelly would be arrested and though initially sentenced to death, he was reprieved, declared insane and admitted to Broadmoor Criminal Lunatic Asylum in Berkshire.

By 23 January 1888, Kelly had escaped, aided by a key he had made from a piece of metal found within the grounds. Once free he remained at large for thirty-nine years.

During his liberty Kelly travelled greatly through Europe and America. On two occasions, while on the run, he had wished to give himself up but decided against it. By 1927 Kelly was suffering ill health. Now aged 67, he was mentally weak, malnourished and completely deaf. Wishing to end his days among friends, Kelly gave himself up and returned to Broadmoor Asylum, dying two years later of pneumonia.

Importantly, James Kelly was at large for the duration of the Ripper murders. The method adopted in the killing of his wife was similar, though not identical, to the Ripper's signature. Unlike some suspects, Kelly knew the area of the East End and often frequented the taverns and inns of Whitechapel. He was also known to associate with prostitutes and at some point had contracted a venereal disease.

One author claims that Kelly admitted to being the Ripper whilst in Broadmoor, while another believes that whilst on the run he was responsible for murders in both England and America.

But if Kelly was the Ripper what was his motive?

History tells us that Kelly was a brute, whose temper was at times uncontrollable. He would verbally and physically abuse his wife and by June 1883 had threatened her with a knife at least twice, the second occasion leading to the murder. Kelly himself would later confirm the belief that he was in fact insane. Whether such insanity could lead to other murders of the nature of the Ripper remains to be seen.

What is certain is that on 10 November 1888, after the discovery of the Ripper's fifth victim, detectives were deployed to Kelly's former residence to conduct a raid and were attempting, though in vain, to locate him. Looking back upon the case and the actions of the police, it appears that Kelly was seen as a possible suspect, at least for a while, and even today must be considered among the most credible.

Tumblety

On 23 September 1913, Detective Chief Inspector John Littlechild of the Metropolitan Police wrote a letter to journalist George Robert Sims. In it he mentioned the Ripper case and the story of an American quack doctor – a 'Dr T.' – who Littlechild believed was a very likely suspect.

Littlechild suggested the existence of a large dossier compiled in relation to a Dr Tumblety. The chief inspector confirmed that as well as being a regular visitor to London, the doctor had also been arrested in 1888. After jumping bail he had fled Britain for Boulogne and soon disappeared to never be heard of again. After this time there were no further Ripper murders.

Littlechild's observations make for interesting reading and when the letter was discovered in 1993 it appeared that finally we had in our midst a plausible candidate.

But who was Dr T.?

Throughout the 1850s, Irish-born Francis Tumblety had made a name for himself in America as an Indian herb doctor. In his youth he had engaged in a plethora of occupations, until eventually setting up business in Detroit as a physician, having gained medical knowledge at Lispenard's Hospital where he had worked.

By 1858 Tumblety had made a small fortune through the sale of his patented medical cures and inventions and was known for his eccentric lifestyle. Unbeknownst to his patients, however, Francis Tumblety was no doctor. In 1860 he was responsible for the death of a patient named James Portmore, who died in agony due to certain potions that Tumblety had prescribed him. Tumblety was arrested and would later be found guilty on a charge of manslaughter, though by the time of the verdict he had vanished.

Five years later Tumblety was arrested again, accused of involvement in the assassination of President Abraham Lincoln due to his association with one of the men directly responsible. A month later Tumblety would again walk free, having had his charge of complicity quashed.

By 1881 he was arrested for pickpocketing in New Orleans and after seven years found himself in the hands of the police once again, this time on a charge of gross indecency. The latter would prove an important moment in the story of Francis Tumblety, for it occurred not in New Orleans or even the United States, but instead in London, England in the summer of 1888.

Tumblety was a great traveller and by his own admission had ventured to the East End during the period of the Ripper murders due to his interest in the case. During his stay he regularly came to the attention of the police, being accused throughout July, August and October of acts of gross indecency, until his eventual arrest on 7 November for four such offences.

Some theorists believe that after his arrest he may have been remanded for up to two weeks, while others suggest that more likely Tumblety was given bail. Tumblety himself would confirm that he had been detained for several days. Either way, by 14 November Tumblety was back in custody and within two days was charged at Marlborough Police Court. He was set bail, with his trial planned for later in the month. What the Metropolitan Police didn't know was that this was to be the last they would ever see of 'Dr T.'.

Tumblety disappeared, first to France, where he travelled under an assumed name, and then on to New York. Once back in America press interest soon began, finding reporters eager to explore Tumblety's association with the Ripper crimes. For a while the American police also appeared interested in Tumblety's activities and kept him under observation.

On reviewing the evidence though, it seems that Littlechild's belief wasn't shared by his American counterparts or many of his colleagues. Should Tumblety have been considered a probable suspect it seems inconceivable that he should be granted bail and when Scotland Yard became aware of his arrival in America, rather than pursuing Tumblety, they showed little interest in locating him.

Tumblety would die in 1903 in St Johns Hospital, St Louis, aged 73. Due to him having spent a lifetime courting the press his death was covered greatly by the newspapers who eagerly exposed the details of his wealth.

As a Ripper suspect it is clear to see why Francis Tumblety should be placed above many other names. Here we have a suspect who was in Whitechapel at the time of the murders. He was suspected by a number of officers as being involved in the Ripper killings, had some degree of medical knowledge and was said to have a hatred of prostitutes.

Yet, as convincing as the evidence appears, there is one element of the Francis Tumblety story that doesn't fit. In physical appearance he differs remarkably from the witness statements of those who saw the Ripper: a man in his 20s or 30s, tall, thin and of respectable demeanour. By 1888 Tumblety was in his late 50s, wore military regalia and was described as being huge in stature and having a peculiarly large moustche.

The charges faced by Tumblety while in London were against men rather than women and should he have been remanded after his arrest he would have been in custody when the Ripper struck on 9 November 1888.

Dr Francis Tumblety remains one of the most interesting suspects to be put forward in recent years and continues to garner interest. Whether he was the Ripper or not remains a mystery.

Maybrick

When in 1991 a diary was discovered in which the writer claimed he was Jack the Ripper it seemed, for a time, that the great hunt was finally over.

At first everything about the diary appeared to fit. Though the diarist gave no name, the clues as to his identity were there to be seen and soon its author was named as successful Liverpudlian cotton merchant James Maybrick.

Prior to the diary's discovery, Maybrick's name was already known to crime historians due to the circumstances surrounding his death in 1889. It was believed that Maybrick's wife Florence had poisoned him with arsenic while at their home in Liverpool. She was arrested and convicted of his murder and the trial that followed went on to capture the interest of a nation.

Florence was sentenced to hang but this was commuted to life imprisonment until her release in 1904, after a re-evaluation of her case.

The dairy was found by Michael Barrett, who stated that an old friend had given it to him. After placing the document in the hands of Rupert Grew Literary Agency, a mass of research was undertaken to prove its provenance.

Maybrick was discovered to be addicted to arsenic, as confirmed in the diary. He was a womaniser and had a young American wife who had been involved in an affair with fellow cotton merchant. As stated in the diary, this affair would be the reason for Maybrick committing his murders. Unable to inflict pain on the woman

James Maybrick and his wife. Did he write the infamous diary? (THP)

he loved, he took out his rage on the prostitutes of the East End. Although, like Tumblety, Maybrick was older than the perceived age of the Ripper, he matched the description of at least one eyewitness.

Under analysis, though the document and its ink were of the period, cracks soon began to appear in the story. Within the entries many errors were found that differed from the known facts relating to the Ripper. The handwriting was different to that of James Maybrick and when, in 1995, Michael Barrett admitted to forging the document, all confidence in the diary was lost. And though he would later rebut this statement, the damage was done.

The diary remains a hot topic and has become possibly the most discussed find in the history of the case. It continues to divide opinion and while it appears likely to be a forgery, the possibility of Maybrick being the Ripper continues to be debated.

Walter

In 1888 a book was printed in Amsterdam titled *My Secret Life*. It was the first of a series of memoirs that detailed the sexual experiences of a Victorian gentleman, exploring a dark and secret world of erotica within nineteenth-century London.

The works encompassed eleven volumes and were written by an author known only as 'Walter'; a fetishist and womaniser who, if his memoirs are to be believed, was also a sexual sadist. Researchers have pointed out that Walter appears to have known at least one of the Ripper's victims, as he describes liaisons with a Mary Davis, in which he provides details of her age, appearance and accommodation that match Mary Kelly, who was also known to some as Mary Davies/Davis.

Walter was in Whitechapel in 1888 and writes of excursions into the East End in which he would dress in shabby attire and spend nights drinking in smoke-laden pubs, surrounded by labourers and prostitutes.

At other times Walter would pass himself off as a doctor. He was also an experienced hunter and was familiar with the use of a knife.

If the memoirs are true then in Walter we certainly find a disturbed and highly dangerous man at large in London at the time of the murders. Is this enough to make him a suspect? The answer must ultimately lie in the true identity of the author of *My Secret Life*. And while many names have been proposed, the real Walter remains as elusive today as the Ripper himself.

Cutbush

On 9 March 1891, 25-year-old Thomas Hayne Cutbush was arrested while attempting to enter his family home in Kennington.

Cutbush was a wanted man. After absconding from Lambeth Infirmary, where he had been detained at the request of his family, he had attacked two women with a knife. After his arrest Cutbush was due to stand trial but ultimately was deemed insane and thus, like James Kelly, was removed to Broadmoor Asylum. He was admitted as patient X32007 on the 23 April 1891 and, but for the actions of one man, the story of Thomas Cutbush would have ended there.

Had it not been for Inspector William Race the truth about Cutbush and his connections to the Ripper case would never have been known.

Race was a highly experienced officer who had assisted in the hunt for the Ripper in 1888. In 1891 he was assigned the task of locating Cutbush and on his arrest began to see distinct similarities between his prisoner and the very man he had pursued in Whitechapel.

As Race delved into Cutbush's past, the inspector became convinced he had caught the Ripper. So sure was Race of his convictions that he would eventually lay his findings before Scotland Yard in the hope that a thorough investigation would be permitted.

Although the investigation never came, Race was unrelenting. He gave information to *The Sun* newspaper and three years later the truth about Cutbush was eventually made public, with the evidence against him seemingly overwhelming.

Living in Kennington with his mother and aunt in 1888, Cutbush had become well acquainted with Whitechapel, having found work in a number of locations in the East End. To some Cutbush appeared simply as a respectable young man; however, hidden behind a veil of normality was another personality entirely.

As confirmed by those who knew him, Cutbush associated with prostitutes and appeared to hold hatred towards women. He believed he had contracted syphilis and would later be described as a disturbed man of filthy habits. Cutbush also studied anatomy and surgery and wished to be seen by others as a doctor, referring to himself as a medical man from London.

It would transpire that Cutbush was regularly sacked from his employment and, when not at home, would spend the dark hours walking the streets of London, returning in the early hours covered in mud and blood.

Cutbush's room would eventually be searched. Found stuffed up a chimney were items of clothing, bloodstained and laced with turpentine, ready to be burnt. Drawings were also discovered, depicting mutilated women.

While at times he could appear quiet and inoffensive, Cutbush was capable of great violence. As well as assaulting a workmate and threatening to kill his doctor, Cutbush had previously attacked a prostitute and a servant, and attempted to slit his mother's throat.

Cutbush escaped from Lambeth Infirmary on 5 March by knocking down his orderlies and vaulting a boundary wall. He was at large for four days, during which time every police station in London was informed of his escape and instructed to apprehend him. While free, Cutbush stabbed one female and attempted to assault another.

During his time at large Cutbush also made a startling confession, stating that he was wanted for a 'grave and serious charge' and announcing that he was believed to be Jack the Ripper. Cutbush insisted upon his innocence before admitting he had only been 'cutting up girls and laying them out'.

Importantly, Cutbush matches the appearance of the Ripper and it was also confirmed that it had been impossible to ascertain his movements on the nights of the Whitechapel Murders. Interestingly, Cutbush also resembles the description of a man seen fleeing Whitechapel on the morning of the discovery of Mary Kelly's body. This male appears to have been seen twice, on both occasions stained with blood, the first sighting occurring in close proximity to Miller's Court and the second taking place in Kennington only streets away from Cutbush's home.

After his admission to Broadmoor the Ripper murders came to an end. Once inside he was kept under close observation, with his warders noting his growing mania and violent tendencies. They also observed his obsession with obtaining a knife and noted that he wished to 'rip-up' those around him. Cutbush was also heard speaking in his room – though he was alone – and believed he was being poisoned. During his confinement Cutbush attacked a fellow patient and on one occasion attempted to bite his mother's face during a visit.

Unlike the Ripper, Cutbush didn't kill his victims – yet he showed a capability for extreme violence. He attacked while on the run, which indicates a desire to maim regardless of the consequences, and significantly Cutbush mirrors the behaviour of many serial killers, in which, by his own admission, he links himself to the murder investigation.

On 5 July 1903, Thomas Cutbush died of chronic kidney failure and with his passing a tragic life, scarred by madness, violence and perhaps even murder, came to a painful end.

Legacy

Some theorists believe we will never know the Ripper's true identity and that the culprit will forever remain in hiding. Yet with the passing of time countless discoveries have been made by dedicated researchers that prove that, as old as the story may be, there is still more to be learnt about the Ripper and his crimes.

Although until now he may have evaded detection, one thing is certain: as long as there is interest in the Whitechapel murder case, the hunt for Jack the Ripper will continue.

Bibliography

Evans, Stewart and Paul Gainey, *Jack the Ripper: First American Serial Killer* (New York: Kodansha America Inc., 1996)

Harrison, Shirley, *The Diary of Jack the Ripper (Index)* (Middlesex: Smith Gryphon Ltd, 1993)

Hodgson, Peter, *Through The Mists of Time* (Kent: Pneuma Springs Publishing, 2011)

Marriott, Trevor, *Jack the Ripper: The 21st Century Investigation* (London: John Blake Publishing Ltd, 2007)

Monaghan, David and Nigel Cawthorne, *Jack the Ripper's Secret Confession: The Hidden Testimony of Britain's First Serial Killer* (London: Constable, 2010)

Paley, Bruce, *Jack the Ripper: The Simple Truth* (Chicago: Trafalgar Square Publishing, 1997)

Sugden, Philip, *The Complete History of Jack the Ripper* (London: Robinson Publishing, 1994)

Tully, James, *The Secret of Prisoner 1167: Was This Man Jack the Ripper?* (London: Robinson Publishing Ltd, 1997)

12

The Establishment: What About The Toffs?

Alan Hunt

Great Britain! The name that at the latter end of the nineteenth century stood throughout the civilised and uncivilised world for all that was seen as moral, virtuous, industrious and inventive, with Queen Victoria as a figurehead for all to see as the paragon of all that was right with the empire. Since the death of her consort, Prince Albert, in 1861, she had become a virtual recluse, but by the time of her golden jubilee in 1887, Victoria was once again in the public eye and leading the nation. It was only a year later though that the murderous rampage in Whitechapel caused concern amongst not only the general populous but the country's establishment as well, unsettling the halls of government and royal residences alike.

Leading up to the 1880s, the upper class were travelling the world becoming ambassadors and foreign administrators, while the middle classes were making business deals and opening factories across the Continent – becoming extremely rich on the proceeds. Even the working classes saw increases in the working wage and standard of living, leading to better living conditions than ever before. But all this also led to another layer of populous at the very bottom of the pile, the poor, unemployed and destitute that seemed to gravitate to the slum areas of big cities, especially London's East End where Whitechapel was the most well known. Here they mixed with Polish, German and Russian Jewish immigrants fleeing persecution from Tsarist Russia and what was thought to be pockets of terrorists hell-bent on overthrowing capitalism. But probably the most worrying aspect of the area was the widespread alcoholic abuse and prostitution rife in the environs of the East End, giving rise to brutality and crime that, although commonplace, became sensational when the Whitechapel Murders took place.

Journalism

This was fuelled by the new medium of tabloid journalism. All the publicity in national and foreign media highlighted the plight of the East End and its social dilemmas to the rest of the world that had, up until then, envied Britain's sense of justice and morality. The knowledge of illicit drinking houses, flop and dosshouses, slum landlords, opium dens and wanton violence most certainly worried the establishment and shone a poor light on the problems in the eye of international opinion. The murders became a source of wonderment for virtually every newspaper across the whole world. It saw journalists flocking to the area to sample what was seen as a sinkhole of depravity and degradation that spawned a madman who showed that all was not well in this civilised utopia. After all, one of the letters attributed to the murderer named the address of origin as 'From Hell'.

Reform

Social reform was rife at this time, with people like Dr Barnado and Charles Booth highlighting the plight of the East End. Meanwhile, W.T. Stead used his editorials – and lost his liberty – in publicising the problem of child prostitution, with works like *The Bitter Cry of Outcast London* by the Revd Andrew Mearns.

But the good meaning was also hijacked by unscrupulous individuals with their own agendas. One such was MP Henry Hyndburn, a Socialist reformer who, using the plight of laid-off dockworkers (after a particularly fierce winter caused canals and harbours to freeze over), organised a demonstration in Trafalgar Square. After a rousing speech he pronounced, 'Follow me to the West End to demand work, bread or blood!' This they did in their hundreds until they came to the Carlton club in St James, where a member made an offensive gesture to the mob, causing them to attack the windows and door then destroy a wine shop next door. After the police came, Hyndburn was arrested and charged with inciting a riot and sent for trial at the Old Bailey. At the trial he defended himself and called on all the witnesses he could, forcing the plight of the impoverished and poor to become front-page news and embarrass the government. He was eventually found not guilty and released to continue his crusade.

Bloody Sunday

All this just a year after the Bloody Sunday riots in the same square, when a demonstration was organised against unemployment, coercion in Ireland and the release of MP William O'Brian – imprisoned for incitement during the recent Irish Land War. Police battled with the mob and around 400 people were arrested with over seventy seriously injured. The man deemed as the villain in this case was Sir Charles Warren, commissioner of the Metropolitan Police, for his use of over 4,000 police officers to quell the riot as well as 300 infantry and 600 lifeguards and mounted police. Warren was to resign from the police just before the murder of Mary Kelly, and was used as a scapegoat for the lack of progress in the murders.

Even the police became embroiled in controversy because of the establishment's paranoia when, in 1887, Elizabeth Cass was arrested and imprisoned after a police constable swore she was a woman he had tried to arrest before for prostitution. She was only a normal housewife out Saturday shopping and her treatment by the authorities on the word of the constable became a scandal; the home secretary, Henry Matthews and the prime minister, Lord Salisbury, were especially condemned.

Discrimination

Not only was there sexual discrimination, but social discrimination too. With the spread of industrial wealth amongst the middle classes came the belief of superiority to both the upper and working classes, giving rise to a deep resentment not only from the poor and impoverished but the working classes also. The upper class also began to resent the vast amount of wealth and power being exerted and flaunted in their faces; many stately homes were being bought up by the new breed of wealthy middle-class industrialists and factory owners.

The personification of the social divide was never more obvious than in the case of Henry Hutt. In the early part of 1888 a scandal arose at Haileybury Prep School, just north of London, when 13-year-old Hutt was accused of stealing money from other boys. As the son of a country vicar and at the school on a scholarship, he was picked on by the headmaster because of his social class and expelled without an inquiry. His father sued the school in the high court with the help of legal friend Charles Russell, son of the eminent Victorian judge Lord Russell. The case was found in the boy's favour and he was reinstated and awarded the sum of £100 in compensation, but the newspapers pursued the sensational case because a number of sons of well-known politicians and figures of the establishment also boarded there.

Foreign policy

Throughout Victoria's reign, Britain's foreign policy had long been seen as pivotal to her well-being, with victories against the Russians in the Crimea in 1855; the Indian mutiny in 1858; the Ashanti nation in 1874; control of Egypt and the Suez canal in 1875; brokering a peace between Russia and the Austro-Hungary empire in 1878, which led to the gaining of Cyprus; and the defeat of the Zulu nation in 1879–80. To this end there was always a suspicion of foreign incursion into Britain, so any notion of foreign involvement in the murders would have set alarm bells ringing in Whitehall and beyond.

The Irish problem

Not only this, but the ever-present Irish problem was intensifying. Home Rule was still an aim for the Fenian brotherhood, a precursor of the IRA, to the extent that several bombings occurred – including the bombing of Scotland Yard and attempted bombing of the Royal Observatory at Greenwich. Unfortunately, an incident in America involving the British ambassador, the presidential election and the Charles Parnell letters didn't help Anglo-Irish relations. The presidential campaign of 1888 saw the Democratic president, Grover Cleveland, under pressure from Republican's opponents, who started to write letters to public figures for information about the president. One such letter went to the British ambassador Sir Henry Sackville-West, asking for his opinion as to how the author should vote, as he was an English-born American. Sackville-West declined to comment on his choice but did say, 'Mr Cleveland, I believe, is still desirous of maintaining friendly relations with Great Britain.' This was immediately pounced upon by the large Irish-American population and other groups with axes to grind against the British, leading to Sackville-West having his credentials cancelled and being sent home in disgrace.

The Parnell incident came about after letters were published signed by Parnell, MP of the moderate Irish Nationalists, stating that he supported the murder in 1882 of Secretary of Ireland Lord Cavendish and his personal secretary Henry Burk in Phoenix Park, Dublin. They also stated that other members of the party supported various acts of violence against British officials. Parnell vehemently refuted the allegations and signatures as forgeries and demand an inquiry. The inquiry sat for 128 days and produced a thirty-five-volume report supporting Parnell and naming the culprit as a journalist, Richard Piggott.

The workers

With the rapid rise in industrialisation in cities and towns, one of the major problems was workers' rights and conditions which, left to continue, could well have caused widespread unrest towards the

The Bryant & May matchgirls' strike was due to the poor working conditions.
(© *The Illustrated London News*, 1871)

middle and upper classes. Probably the most famous of these was the Bryant & May matchgirls' strike which started with an article in the *Link Newspaper* by Annie Besant, deploring the working conditions and treatment of workers by the management in the factory. To counter this, the factory manager drew up a letter refuting the allegations and demanded three girls from the shop floor to put their names to it. This they refused to do and were immediately sacked, which led to the entire 1,200 workforce walking out on strike.

Numerous societies and newspapers took up their cause and raised funds to help the workers. Charles Bradaugh, an East End MP, invited a group of the girls to parliament to meet other members and discuss their plight. The company eventually gave in to the girls' grievances and improved their conditions, which showed that public opinion and a well-organised workforce were able to force draconian management styles to change. This was probably the first workers' union and caused consternation amongst the wealthy factory owners, businessmen and investors who held the country's economic reins, especially as they already held the threat of communism in the back of the minds.

Women

Also starting to voice their grievances were the women of Britain, often seen as mere housekeepers to their spouses and children. Mona Caird, in an article in the *Westminster Review Magazine*, labelled marriage for life as a 'Vexatious Failure' and gave examples of laws that worked against the interest of women. She also advocated changes to the divorce laws, which would make it easier for couples to part with fairer settlements for both parties. The article caused an outcry throughout the country with newspapers, the church and the public debating the pros and cons of the laws. Several newspapers began printing letters from various sources for and against the reforms, with *The Daily Telegraph* receiving over 27,000 on the subject, and it stayed on the front pages until the Autumn of Terror in Whitechapel stole the headlines.

Violence

But there was always the ever-present danger of violence and brutality associated with the perils of poverty and alcohol. Domestic violence was on the increase amongst the downtrodden and murders were becoming commonplace in areas such as Whitechapel and the East End, connected so closely to the London Docks and its proximity to drinking houses and opium dens. The year before, a strange murder case came to the attention of the police and the public. A man was walking his dog along the side of the Thames at Rainham when he noticed a package floating near the riverbank. Thinking it might be something that had fallen off one of the many cargo ships sailing the river and could be of value, he rescued it. Upon peeling the covering he found the limbless and headless torso of a naked woman. Later on further parcels were found floating, holding the severed limbs, but there was no sign of the head, the only real way of identifying the victim. A police surgeon, Dr Thomas Bond, who was later to play a major part in the Whitechapel Murders, examined the torso and stated that although the dismemberment was made by someone with knowledge of anatomy it was not necessarily a doctor. A butcher or a knacker could conceivably have done it, echoing the later Ripper investigation. As no one was reported missing in the area, the case has remained open ever since.

Scandal

Even the wealth and influence enjoyed by the very highest levels of society couldn't grant immunity to scandal or intrigue. For a long time, Victoria had been despairing of her eldest son, Edward

Prince Albert Victor, who
became embroiled in the
Cleveland Street Scandal. (THP)

the Prince of Wales, because of his philandering and liaisons
with various ladies of prominent society backgrounds, as well as
actresses from the stage. He became a source of consternation for
both his parents and Victoria even blamed him for the death of
his father because, although ill, Albert went to reprimand Edward
for a dalliance with the actress Nellie Clifton in Ireland while
there on army manoeuvres. He was also implicated in the divorce
proceedings of a prominent MP, Sir Charles Mordaunt, as he was
known to visit his wife while the MP was away at Parliament. He was
never called to the witness box but the rumours were widespread.
Lillie Langtry, Sarah Bernhardt and Sophie Keppel were three of
his known mistresses but there were numerous more.

Matters were worsened by Edward's eldest son, Prince Albert
Victor, becoming just as much of a problem as his father. Apart from
his alleged connection with the Ripper murders (which has never
been proved) he became embroiled with what became to be known
as the Cleveland Street Scandal.

The Cleveland Street Scandal

In 1889 it came to light that a homosexual brothel was operating from the premises of the GPO telegraph office at No. 19 Cleveland Street Fitzrovia, central London. At the time, homosexual acts were illegal between men and punishable by imprisonment and the undoubted social ostracism that would follow. Police were called in to investigate when telegraph boys were found to have large amounts of money on them against post office rules; it turned out they were indulging in sexual acts with various prominent figures for money. Inspector Frederick Abberline, well known from the Ripper case a year earlier, headed the investigation, which resulted in the arrest of four telegraph boys: Charles Thomas Swingscow, Henry Newlove, George Alma Wright and Charles Ernest Thickbroom. A man was named as their controller, Charles Hammond, but he fled to the Continent after being warned by Newlove of the investigation. As for the clients, none were arrested or charged, but Newlove named Lord Arthur Somerset, equerry to the Prince of Wales, and Henry Fitzroy, Earl of Euston, amongst others. Because of Somerset's position as equerry, rumours abounded that a member of the Royal Family was involved and the prince was the main suspect, compounded by Somerset's solicitor threatening to name him. Eventually only Newlove and another boy, Henry Veck, were charged and they received five- and three-month prison sentences respectively. This was seen as extraordinarily lenient of the courts, accused of covering up the scandal because of the high-ranking persons involved, another cause of resentment.

It later turned out that Hammond's passage to the Continent was paid for by Somerset's solicitor Newton, and neither Hammond nor Somerset were to be extradited on the orders of Prime Minister Lord Salisbury. This gave rise to the feeling that male homosexuality, although illegal, was rife amongst the aristocracy. Eventually Newton rather blotted his own copybook; in 1913 he was suspended from the bar for falsifying letters in the defence of Dr Hawley Harvey Crippen for the murder of his wife.

Revolution

No doubt the 1888 events in Whitechapel caused concern for every layer of society above the very lowest strata. It threatened the class system they benefited from and reminded them of the danger of the residents of the East End rising up against their sorry treatment to plunge the country into anarchy. But that never really came into being.

Whether it was the publicity given to the murders or the realisation that conditions had to be changed for the better, Britain seemed to retreat from the edge of social revolution. It instead strove for ever more prosperous avenues to better its people's way of life and eradicate the spectre of abject poverty that had blighted Britain for so long. Margaret Harkness, writing under the name John Law, wrote a book titled *In Darkest London*. In it she warned: 'The whole of the East End is starving. The West End is bad, or mad, not to see that if things go on like this we must have a revolution. One fine day the people about here will go desperate, and they will walk westwards, cutting throats and hurling brickbats, until they are shot down by the military!'

A fair warning heeded by those in authority, I believe.

13

Jack The Ripper: The Letters

Christopher Jones

Dear Bass,

You have not found me yet I have done another one and thrown it in the river and I mean doing another one before the weeks out. You can put as many blood hounds as you like but you will never catch me.

Yours truly

Jack Ripper

This postcard was sent on 5 October 1888 to Sir Charles Warren, the police commissioner who had ultimate responsibility for overseeing the investigation of the Ripper murders. One of the features of these murders is the large number of letters received by the police, the press and various other groups and individuals, many of which claimed to have been written by the killer. Most of these letters were from cranks and simply wasted a great deal of police time.

Helpful advice?

To the Editor of *The Times* [printed 11 September 1888]

Sir, – I would suggest that the police should at once find out the whereabouts of all cases of 'homicidal mania' which may have been discharged as 'cured' from metropolitan asylums during the last two years.

Your obedient servant, A Country Doctor

Not all the letters came from cranks; many came from people who were simply trying to help the police in their enquiries. The letter from 'A Country Doctor' was published just days after the murder of Annie Chapman and people were already linking her death to the murders of Polly Nichols and Martha Tabram. The fact that the victims had been mutilated suggested that the killer might be mentally deranged and the day after that letter was printed, *The Times* printed another letter containing a similar opinion from Dr Forbes Winslow, a man who had experience of dealing with mentally ill patients. He suggested that the police looked for someone from the 'upper class of society' and that 'the murders have been committed by a lunatic lately discharged from some asylum, or by one who has escaped'. Rather ironically, a letter sent two weeks later to the authorities actually suggested Dr Forbes Winslow as a potential suspect as he appeared to the writer to have 'a very peculiarly constituted mind'.

Dr Forbes Winslow. (THP)

Less than helpful advice!

To the City Police [3 October 1888]

No one seems to think of the possibility of the slayer of the six women at Whitechapel being other than a man, but it may be in fact woman or neither one nor the other. It may be a large animal of the Ape species belonging to some wild beast show.

Mrs L. Painter (Burlington Lodge, Ryde)

Several letters made suggestions on how the killer was able to avoid detection. Mrs L. Painter, who felt that the killer might be a wild beast, also informed the City police that she believed that such an animal would be 'swift, cunning, noiseless and strong' and that it could disappear in a moment 'high up in a tree or other safe place'. Some slightly more plausible suggestions sent to the police were that the killer escaped through the London's sewers or that he was a watchman and therefore could walk unnoticed through the streets at night.

Common advice

To the City Police [6 October 1888]

Is there no one there [at London Hospital] doing clerking &c. who has acquired a little surgical knowledge. May have watched the use of the knife. May have access [to] certain knives and possibly drugs may know how to keep the victims silent by pressure on certain nerves in the neck.

(Unsigned)

Many of the letters that were sent to the police contained similar pieces of advice. The fact that the murderer appeared to possess some skill with the knife led many to suggest someone with some medical knowledge or experience. One unsigned letter to the City police suggested that they carry out a thorough search of London Hospital in an effort to identify people who may have acquired some surgical skills. Another common suggestion was that he could be a butcher or a slaughterman, especially a Jewish slaughterman.

To the Editor of The Times [1 October 1888]

Sir. – I beg to suggest the organisation of a small force of plain-clothes constables mounted on bicycles for the rapid and noiseless patrolling of streets and roads by night.

Your obedient servant, Fred Wellesley (Merton Abbey, Surrey)

The most popular suggestion found in the letters was the proposal that police officers should be armed and disguised as women. Another one was that a special force of constables on bicycles should be created who could move swiftly around the streets of London. The idea that silent movement could be the key to apprehending the killer was expressed in other letters. A certain L.R. Thomson wrote to *The Times* in October 1888, recommending that all police boots 'should be furnished with a noiseless sole or rubber heel … to prevent the sound of their measured tread being heard at night'. Further suggestions included the use of bloodhounds, improved street lighting and offering a substantial reward. Henry White, the magistrate of Middlesex, wrote to the newspapers in October 1888 that 'a large reward, say £1,000, should at once be offered'. He even offered to put £50 towards the cost of the reward.

Policing the police

To Sir Charles Warren [18 October 1888]

The policeman Watkins that found the body of the woman in Mitre Square I want you to keep an eye on him you may think it strange I should pick out a man in the service but if he was in the police service or my own brother I would for the sake of the people try and find out Dear Sir if he should be the man.

(Unsigned)

That the killer was proving impossible to catch led many letter writers to suggest that he might have been a police officer or someone dressed up as an officer. One letter sent to the city commissioner speculated that the killer might be a 'human fiend in the disguise of a policeman'. Another letter suggested PC Watkins as a potential suspect; he was the constable who had discovered the body of Catherine Eddowes in Mitre Square.

Such suggestions and any other criticisms of the police were not well received by senior officers. When Sir Charles Warren received a letter from the Chairman of the Board of Works in the Whitechapel District suggesting that police levels needed to be strengthened in the area, he replied with a forceful letter of his own that was published in *The Times*. In the letter he claimed: 'statistics show that London is the safest city in the world to live in' and that a 'large force of police had already been drafted into the Whitechapel District to assist those already there to the full extent necessary to meet the requirement'. As his letter was published only days after the double murder of Stride and Eddowes, his words probably sounded rather hollow to many East End residents. Warren also implied that the reason why the killer hadn't yet been caught was because the 'unfortunate victims appear to take the murderer to some retired spot and to place themselves in such a position that they can be slaughtered without a sound being heard; the murder, therefore, takes place without any clue to the criminal being left'.

Racist stereotypes and foreign suspects

To the Mayor of the city of London [15 October 1888]

> I have long believed the murderer to be a Jew, as I know that a number of Jews believe in the literal meaning of the law as laid down in their Bible, which says that a woman who is a prostitute shall be put to death.
>
> *Alese Brown, Caledonian Place, Aberdeen*

One of the most common rumours circulating in Whitechapel was that the murderer was a Jewish man nicknamed 'Leather Apron' (such as John Pizer). Such rumours provoked both anti-Semitic demonstrations and letters. Mr Brown of Aberdeen, who suggested that the murderer might be a Jew and especially 'a Jewish Minister', claimed that he had worked in Whitechapel and knew the area and the people who lived there very well. If the latter was the case, then his views probably just reflected the racist rumours that were unfortunately widespread at the time.

To the Editor of The Times [4 October 1888]

> Sir, – Having been long in India and, therefore, acquainted with the methods of Eastern criminals, it has struck me in reading the accounts of these Whitechapel murders that they have probably been committed by a Malay, or other low class Asiatic coming under the general term Lascar [an Indian sailor], of whom, I believe there are large numbers in that part of London.
>
> *Your obedient servant, NEMO*

It wasn't just Jews who were accused of being the Ripper; Whitechapel was home to people from many ethnic backgrounds and the finger of suspicion was often pointed at foreigners and immigrants. The fact that the victims were mutilated further reinforced the idea that the murderer was foreign as such acts were considered to be inherently alien practices. The letter writer who pointed the finger at a Malay immigrant wrote that 'cutting off the nose and ears, ripping up the body, and cutting out certain organs are all peculiarly Eastern methods'. Foreigners who had some medical expertise were viewed as especially suspicious. One Bristol resident wrote to the City police in October 1888 informing them of his suspicions about an American doctor who had lived and worked in the city. The writer felt that the doctor resembled the composite sketch of the Ripper suspect that had appeared in *The Daily Telegraph*.

Suspects named

To the City Police Commissioner [6 October 1888]

There is a poor lunatic named Herbert Freund who has been in the hands of police several times for disturbances in St. Paul's. I do not know anything whatever against this man, whom I have never seen, except that he was educated for a doctor and he went mad on the subject of religion.

John Bland, Sinclair Road, Kensington, London

Many of the letters sent to the police actually provided a name for the alleged murderer. One such letter, sent by a certain John Bland of Kensington, suggested that the Ripper was a lunatic named Herbert Freund. This suggestion is interesting as Bland's theory combined several of the ideas that were prevalent at the time, namely that the killer had some medical expertise, was insane and that he was driven by a powerful religious zeal.

Liverpool letter

Liverpool 29th inst.

Beware I shall be at work on the 1st and 2nd Inst, in the Minories at twelve midnight, and I give the authorities a good chance, but there is never a policeman near when I am at work.

Yours Jack the Ripper
Prince William St., L'pool.

What fools the police are. I even give them the name of the street where I am living.

The letters that were sent to the press and the police came from all over the country and not just London. One such letter that has attracted a lot of attention is the so-called 'Liverpool letter'. This letter has led people to speculate that the killer may have lived not in Whitechapel but in another part of the country such as Liverpool.

Dear Boss letter

Although hundreds of anonymous letters were sent to the police from writers claiming to be the Ripper, most of them can be easily dismissed; however, two of them have attracted a great deal of interest. The first of these is known as the Dear Boss letter as it was addressed: 'Dear Boss, Central News Office, London City'. It had a London East Central postmark, dated 27 September 1888, was written in red ink in a mocking tone and signed 'Jack the Ripper'. The editor thought it was hoax and waited two days before passing it to the police. The letter refers to a previous murder, presumably Annie Chapman, and it contained the threat to 'clip the lady's ears off' in the next murder. A few days later, a second message written in red crayon on a postcard was sent to the Central News Agency. Again it had an East London postmark and was dated 1 October. Although the handwriting wasn't exactly the same, the words Boss, Squeal and, of course, Jack the Ripper, make it possible that both letters were written by the same person. It read:

I was not codding dear old Boss when I gave you the tip. You'll hear about Saucy Jack's work tomorrow. Double event this time. Number one squealed a bit. Couldn't finish straight off. Had not time to get ears off for police. Thanks for keeping last letter back till I got to work again.

Jack the Ripper

The postcard was passed to the police, who put the two documents together and thought that they may have come from the murderer. As a result, they released facsimiles copies to the press and asked if anyone recognised the handwriting. This action only added to the hysteria surrounding the murders and provided the killer with the infamous name of Jack the Ripper. Even worse, the publicity surrounding the release of the letters proved counterproductive and the police were quickly flooded with copycat letters that wasted both their time and energy.

American Ripper

The reference to cutting the ears and the dates the letters were received led many people to initially believe that the Dear Boss letter and postcard did come from the murderer. It was further suggested that the letter was penned by an American as the term 'Boss' is an American word.

Journalist Ripper

Despite these initial views, both Robert Anderson and Melville Macnaghten, two senior police officers at Scotland Yard, believed that the letter was actually written by journalists.

Anderson even claimed to know who the journalist was. There are some clues in the letter that point to the author being literate; for example, all the full stops are in the correct place, there isn't a single spelling mistake and there are no crossings out. Some of the language of the letter, such as 'ripping' and planning to 'clip the lady's ears off' also points more to a journalist trying to milk a story rather than a real murderer glorying in his crimes. As does the letter being addressed to the Central News Agency rather than the police.

Macnaghten. (THP)

The most significant part of the Dear Boss letter and postcard, and the reason why it was taken so seriously by the authorities, was the reference to the 'double event' (i.e. the murders of Stride and Eddowes that took place on the night of 29/30 September). Although the reference is quite striking, some newspapers had carried stories about the murders on Sunday, 30 September and therefore it is possible that a hoaxer, such as a clever journalist, could have simply incorporated the phrase into the card after the murders were committed. Also, neither victim actually had their ears severed, which the writer of the Dear Boss letter had threatened to do. Eddowes did have an ear lobe detached, but considering the extensive mutilation to her face and body, that was hardly significant. Stride had no marks on her ear apart from an old wound.

'From Hell' letter

> From Hell.
> Mr Lusk,
>
>   Sir
>   I send you half the kidne I took from one woman prasarved it for you tother piece I fried and ate it was very nise I may send you the bloody knif that took it out if you wate a whil longer.
>
>   Signed
>   Catch me when
>   you can
>   Mishter Lusk.

The second letter of real significance is known as the 'From Hell' letter. The letter's heading seems to imply that it may have originated from a religious fanatic; however, it contained no religious or satanic content. It was sent to George Lusk, the chairman of the Mile End Vigilance Committee and he received it through the post on the evening of Tuesday, 16 October 1888. It consisted of a small brown parcel wrapped in brown paper; inside the parcel was half a kidney and an addressed note. The kidney was sent to Dr Openshaw, the pathologist curator of the London Hospital Museum, who confirmed that it was a left kidney and that it had come from an adult human. He did not describe it as a 'ginny' kidney from an alcoholic woman, a story which was widely reported at the time. As the kidney was felt to be very similar to the one that remained in Eddowes' body, it was believed that the letter might have actually come from Eddowes' killer. This was not a view shared by Dr Sedgwick Saunders, the City's public analyst, who felt the whole thing was just a hoax by a medical student. Opinion surrounding the origins of the 'From Hell' letter is still disputed by historians; however, of all the anonymous letters sent to the police, it is possibly the only letter that may have come from the actual killer.

Hoaxers who were caught

Although the writers of the Dear Boss and From Hell letters were never caught, the authorities did manage to identify some of the other letter writers who claimed to be the serial killer. One hoaxer was Mary Coroner, who sent her letters to a newspaper in Bradford and to the Chief Constable of Yorkshire stating that Jack the Ripper was on his way to Bradford to 'do a little business'. She was charged on 21 October 1888 with causing a breach of the peace.

Charlotte Higgins, a 14-year-old maid, wrote anonymous letters to her employers, a Devon clergyman and his wife, threatening to cut them up. She was sentenced in December 1888 to three weeks' imprisonment, though for stealing ribbons rather than writing the letters. Miriam Howells sent letters to her friends in a Welsh mining village, signed Jack the Ripper and threatening them with murder. Although the letters were only meant as a prank, not everyone saw the funny side and she ended up before the local magistrates.

The letters keep a-coming

Dear Boss,

Bewware Jack the Ripper is going to commit another murder on the 1st December 1889.

Farewell,
Jack the Ripper

(Addressed to the 'Head Officer' at Scotland Yard
and dated 29 November 1889)

Although the death of Mary Kelly in November 1888 is usually considered the last Ripper murder, anonymous letters were still being received by the police many months after her death. One 'Dear Boss' letter received by the police in October 1896 informed them that the killer had been 'abroad' but was now 'ready to go on with his work'. Thankfully, it proved to be nothing more than a hoax. This letter proved to be one of the last ones sent to the police, for as the murders ended so did they.

Conclusion

Although it is unlikely that any of the letters that were sent to the police claiming to come from the murderer were actually genuine, there are examples of serial killers who have written letters to the police. For example, Peter Kurten, the Dusseldorf murderer who partly modelled himself on Jack the Ripper, wrote letters to the newspapers in the same way that he believed that the Whitechapel killer had done. Therefore, it is possible that one or more of the letters, such as the infamous 'From Hell' letter, were penned by the killer. But whoever sent them, the only group to really benefit from the letters were the newspapers that used them to sensationalise storylines and so boost sales. These storylines in turn acted as a catalyst to produce even more letters.

In truth, the main contributions of the letters, especially the anonymous ones, to the Ripper story were essentially negative, wasting a great deal of police time and stirring up public opinion and hatreds, especially against minority groups such as Jews and foreigners. As for the helpful suggestions the police received, if they had been adopted we might have seen a police force disguised as women with special footwear, bicycles and bloodhounds, searching the better-lit streets for a man, woman or even a wild beast!

14

The Fall Out

Gill Payne

*This chapter is written in memory of David Viney,
my father, who introduced me to a life of crime.*

Why do the Whitechapel Murders cast such a spell in the twenty-first century? They remain unsolved after 125 years and there are still nearly as many suspects, some of them clearly more serious contenders than others. There is also debate about the number of victims; in the 1880s around 200 people were found dead on the streets annually in London – mostly in the East End and, as Catherine Arnold says, 'The deaths of so many prostitutes went unreported that it was impossible to calculate how many of these unfortunate women had not committed suicide but become the victims of a serial killer.' So before we even factor in the mythology of Jack the Ripper we are dealing with shifting sands.

Still alive

Jack the Ripper has become an abiding image of Victorian Gothic alongside the Madwoman in the Attic and the Elephant Man. The events and the lives of some of the protagonists have become corrupted, romanticised, trivialised, tamed and subsumed into the national psyche. Not only has there been a spate of TV series, but I have seen a production of *Jack the Ripper the Musical* at the Minnack Theatre in Cornwall – and who could forget the Two Ronnies serial *The Phantom Raspberry Blower of Olde London Town*?

The Autumn of Terror was the living embodiment of both a sensation novel and a detective story (which were all the rage at the time: *A Study in Scarlet*, the first Sherlock Holmes story, being published the year before). Sara Wise in *The Blackest Streets* sums up the problem perfectly when she talks about 'the fog of journalistic mis-reporting and plain invention that has cloaked so much of the Whitechapel Murders case'. This is just one of the consequences of the Whitechapel Murders but there were many more both in the short and longer term.

As no one was caught in the immediate aftermath, the historical activities of convicted murderers and asylum inmates were reviewed by the police. This is reflected in the Macnaghten memorandum, written in 1894 but not made public until 1959, and an example of the slow reveal of information which keeps the case alive.

Suspects

Another suspect was Severin Klosovski, later known as George Chapman or 'The Borough Poisoner', was a Polish surgeon and barber. He was hanged in 1903 for poisoning three of his wives. Inspector Abberline, quoted in the *Pall Mall Gazette* in 1903, thought Chapman was the Ripper, but it would be unusual for a serial killer to change their modus operandi.

Mary Pearcy – Jill the Ripper?
(© Casebook.org)

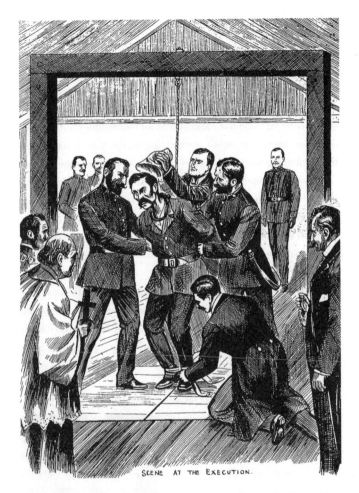

SCENE AT THE EXECUTION.

George Chapman, 'The Borough Poisoner', who was hanged in 1903.
(© *The Illustrated Police News*, 1888)

The conviction of Mary Pearcey raised the possibility of Jill the Ripper. Mary Pearcey was hanged in 1890 for the murder of Phoebe Hogg and her baby daughter, having disposed of their bodies in the streets with the aid of the baby's pram.

The police

Of the police officers involved in the case three are of particular interest. In the short term, Inspector Abbeline of Scotland Yard was transferred to other duties, eventually leaving the Metropolitan Police. Later he worked in Monte Carlo for Pinkerton's, the American detective agency, policing the gaming tables before retiring to Bournemouth, where he died in 1929. He was reckoned to be one of the most conscientious of the detectives at Scotland Yard, but his image has subsequently been corrupted beyond recognition. In the film *From Hell* he is glamorously portrayed by Johnny Depp as a drug user and frequenter of opium dens, another staple of the Victorian Gothic and bearing more relation to Dickens' 'Edwin Drood' than reality.

Sir Charles Warren, recruited to the Metropolitan Police for his military approach and not used to having his decisions subjected to media and public scrutiny, resigned the day before Mary Kelly was murdered. He resumed his military career and, promoted to lieutenant general, went on to fight in the Boer War. He came to grief at the Battle of Spion Kop in 1900, and lost 1,700 infantrymen in the process. However, he is still highly regarded in archaeological circles today. In 1870 'Jerusalem Warren' gained fame for excavating under the Temple mount in Jerusalem, a site of sacred significance to Freemasonary. Warren was then an enthusiastic Freemason, but renounced the order in 1901 for reasons that remain unclear.

Inspector Reid, who replaced Abberline in H Division in 1887, has been immortalised in *Ripper Street* but even in his lifetime he was the inspiration for a series of detective novels by Charles Gibbon. He was interested in ballooning, even making a parachute jump.

Immigration

A wave of Russian, Polish and German Jewish immigrants resulted in a concentration of around 50,000 in Whitechapel by 1888. They were accused not so much of stealing people's jobs, as they brought specialist trades with them, but of taking housing. The Lipski murder in 1887 fuelled suspicion and fear, and it also didn't help that various descriptions of the Ripper referred to his Jewish appearance. Founding their own educational and charitable institutions, there was also a feeling that the Jewish community looked after their own. In 1910, Robert Anderson became involved in an argument in the press for saying the Jewish community knew who the Ripper was but protected him as a fellow Jew.

Preceding the Ashkenazi Jews was a wave of Irish immigrants following the potato famines of the 1840s, although they didn't concentrate solely in the East End: the St Giles rookery was known as 'Little Ireland'. The 1880s marked a bombing campaign by the Fenians against Home Rule, targeting the new Underground service by placing bombs at Charing Cross and Paddington where seventy-two passengers were injured in 1883.

A remark by Douglas G. Browne in 1956, quoted in *Jack the Ripper – Scotland Yard Investigates* states that Macnaghten 'appears to identify the Ripper with the leader of a plot to assassinate Mr Balfour at the Irish Office'. This probably emanates from records that subsequently went missing, but government offices were certainly bombed.

Chief Inspector John Littlechild, head of the Special Irish Branch (later the Special Branch) for ten years, had a particular interest in the Irish-American with Fenian sympathies, Dr Tumblety, who was also a Ripper suspect. There is rumoured to be a large Special Branch dossier on Tumblety 'closed in perpetuity'.

Art

The murders also had an impact on the artistic community, not only throwing up more suspects but also cashing in on events.

Walter Sickert came to attention as a suspect based on his paintings of sleeping or dying prostitutes especially 'Camden Town Murder'. His DNA was found on the back of a stamp suggesting he may have been involved in writing some of the Ripper letters. He is also linked to the Duke of Clarence who was sent to Sickert to develop his artistic appreciation.

Richard Mansfield's nightly metamorphosis from Dr Jekyll to Mr Hyde at the Lyceum in 1888 stoked the hysteria of the Ripper as a monster. As Judith Flanders notes, a playgoer reported him to the police solely on the grounds that 'I do not think there is A man Living So well able to disguise Himself in a moment … Who So well able to Baffel the Police, or Public'.

Even as the murders were occurring, local waxwork shows sprang up featuring effigies of both victims and an imagined perpetrator, as well as a plethora of songs, sketches, melodramas and novels. The early twentieth-century novels *The Lodger* and *Lulu* are examples that were later made into silent films, starring a smouldering Ivor Novello and Louise Brookes respectively.

Abroad

The fear of the Ripper spread abroad rapidly, even as far as America.

Of suspects who spent time in America, Inspector Abberline thought George Chapman could have committed murder during his time there. He is probably referring to the murder of Carrie Brown in April 1891 but the dates do not tally. Ameer Ben Ali was wrongly convicted, sent to Sing Sing and later to Matteawan Asylum. The unsafe conviction was largely due to the bravado of

Thomas F. Byrnes, Chief of the Detective Bureau of the New York police, who said that if Ripper came to USA he would be caught within forty-eight hours.

Dr Neil Cream, actually Scottish, trained as a doctor in Toronto and practised in Chicago. He was in Joliet prison, Illinois, for ten years from 1881 for murdering prostitutes by poisoning. He came to London on his release and went on to poison another four before being executed in 1892. His last-minute confession of being the Ripper is fantasy as he was in prison in America in 1888.

The aforementioned Fenian suspect, Francis Tumblety, 'an American quack', escaped to New York in November 1888 after being arrested for gross indecency with men. Tumblety was reported as having a collection of medical exhibits, including pickled uteri. He was also reported to be hostile towards prostitutes, but both claims were widely disputed by people who knew him.

However, what is not disputed is that Inspector Andrews of Scotland Yard did travel to New York via Toronto and Montreal in December 1888, accompanying two criminals who were being extradited. It is mooted that this trip had some connection with the Whitechapel Murders. Some researchers think Tumblety may have been the Batty Street lodger in the Lipski case, but he was certainly monitored by Chief Inspector Byrnes.

The slow drip feed

As already noted, one of the reasons that keeps interest alive in the Whitechapel Murders is the slow drip feed of new evidence, such as the Macnaghten memorandum. The Swanson annotation naming Kosminski did not come to light until 1987 and the letter written by Chief Inspector John Littlechild to the journalist George Sims, implicating Dr Tumblety, was not discovered by Stewart P. Evans until 1993.

It was not until the 1960s that the Duke of Clarence, known as Prince Eddy, emerged as a suspect. He first rose to attention in a biography about Edward VII and a later article in *The Criminologist*. He is central to the film *From Hell* where his story is developed as a cover up for indiscretion. He had a short but scandalous life, managing to get cited in both the Cleveland Street Scandal in 1889 and as a suspect for the Whitechapel Murders, although he had alibis for each murder. He died at 26, most likely from syphilis, and before he could get into any more trouble.

More recently, in 1992, the Maybrick Diary and watch emerged from uncertain provenance. The diary contains confessional accounts of the five murders as well as two others. Previously, James Maybrick was famous as a victim of poisoning by his wife, Florence, although there is a theory that claims he may have died from the sudden withdrawal of regular drug use. A watch engraved 'I am Jack' and bearing the initials of five victims alongside Maybrick's signature accompanied the diary. The diary has yet to be totally disproved as forensic analysis of ink and paper show them to date to the period, but it is generally regarded as a fake.

Lunatic X32007

The latest example of new evidence is the release of medical records from Broadmoor for 'Lunatic X32007' relating to Thomas Cutbush. David Bullock, in his book *The Man Who Would Be Jack*, makes a persuasive case for Cutbush, the suspect sidelined by the Macnaghten memorandum. He was found guilty of wounding two women and sentenced to Broadmoor for life; this was seen as an unduly harsh sentence at the time, but was this a police cover up to remove the Ripper from society?

David Bullock argues that the case compiled by two *Sun* reporters and Inspector William Race in the 1890s was deliberately downgraded as Cutbush was closely related to a senior police officer. Cutbush's uncle, Charles Henry Cutbush, Head of the Commissioner's Office, subsequently committed suicide.

Forensics

If the Ripper murders happened today we could expect a white tent on the pavement surrounded by striped police tape and maybe a reconstruction on *Crimewatch*. In 1888 there was little concept of preserving the crime scene or of the contamination of evidence. Things had moved on since the murders in the Ratcliffe Highway in 1811, when there was an endless stream of spectators trooping through the house to view the bodies, but sightseers were still charged a penny to look down on the Hanbury Street murder site from next door and food stalls soon arrived to cater for the crowds. Fiona Rule notes how Millers Court attracted both sightseers and entrepreneurs wanting to hire the murder room and buy Mary Kelly's bed.

Even with modern-day forensics, the hunt for a serial killer can be protracted. In 1888 the police made the most of the limited tools available to them. They had photography but these were mainly post-mortem photos except for those of the Mary Kelly crime scene, the only one that could be remotely described as being in a domestic setting. These graphic photos are still horrific and reminiscent of the worst excesses of Hannibal Lecter.

Fingerprinting was not available either, although they had first been suggested as a means of identification in 1880 by Henry Fauld in *Nature* journal. Mark Twain used it as a plot device in *Life on the Mississippi* in 1883 but Galton's Details, the first systematic classification of prints, was not established until 1892 by Francis Galton. The system was refined into individual characteristics by Sir Edward Henry in 1897 and still forms the basis of most of fingerprinting analysis used today.

Profiling

However, what was truly cutting edge was that Dr Bond, the police surgeon at Westminster, was invited to compile what we would now call a profile. In 1989 the FBI came up with a fairly similar description, with the added suggestion that the murderer had probably been questioned by the police at some time but had been plausible enough to be released. The initial search for a monster or an outsider evolved into the more modern concept of looking for somebody who could easily blend in with the background.

Even by 1889, Robert Anderson, talking about spotting criminals generally, said, 'But he won't look any different from any one else'.

In 1888, Dr Winslow, son of a famous alienist and asylum owner, also made his thoughts known to the police. His observations of mental health patients lead him to formulate the characteristics of what we would now call a psychopathic serial killer. His observations led him to name a certain Mr G. Wentworth Bell Smith, a Canadian commercial traveller in trusses, as the killer.

Criminology evolved in the UK, initially as a branch of psychiatry in the early 1920s, but didn't really have any wide-spread influence until the 1950s. There was a huge fear of crime at the time of the murders – but fear of crime did not really come to the notice of criminologists or politicians until the 1970s.

Today

Today Jack the Ripper would be classified as a sexually sadistic serial killer, because he had more than three victims, a distinctive modus operandi, a target victim group and took body parts as trophies. There would be attempts to establish the trigger and motive for the initial murder, because as the sequence progresses murders often become more ritualised and violent. Mental health diagnosis is also more sophisticated now and he would be more likely be diagnosed with an anti-social or narcissistic personality disorder. These days, as is reflected in popular crime fiction, the key to whodunnit is often whydunnit.

Unsanitary and overcrowded

The murders once again highlighted the unsanitary, overcrowded living conditions in the East End. In addition, the poorly lit areas and the absence of officers on the beat were cited as factors that contributed to the murders so one of the immediate responses was to extend gas lighting into the alleyways of Spitalfields and Whitechapel. The area was awash with philanthropic initiatives and there had already been earlier attempts to break up the rookeries by driving through new roads, such as Commercial Street in the 1840s.

Otherwise, little changed until the London County Council (LCC) was founded in 1889. Some outsiders had always had a morbid fascination with the area. The information Dickens gathered on night visits was incorporated into his novels, and organised 'slumming' trips were an after-dinner treat for the middle classes in the 1880s. Sarah Wise notes that at some point both William Beveridge and Clement Atlee visited. Perhaps the conditions they saw influenced the thinking that would eventually lead to the foundation of the Welfare State in 1948.

The new LCC pushed through the Housing of the Working Classes Act in 1890 and took over inspections of the common lodging houses from the police four years later. Slum clearance was prioritised and the somewhat paternalistic Boundary Street Scheme, to replace the Old Nichol, was drawn up as a model of what could be achieved. None of the slum residents were consulted about their needs or desires. Initially designed just to replace the original street layout, the plans were revised into a spacious and pastoral radial design. The rubble from the Old Nichol was used to construct the mound topped by the bandstand in the centre of Arnold Circus. Demolition began in 1893. The profiteering landlords were compensated and 5,719 tenants were evicted. It is somewhat shocking, however, that only eleven could afford to move into the new development.

So in the twenty-first century new evidence is still emerging for researchers and the cultural legacy is flourishing in TV series such as *Whitechapel*, *Ripper Street* and a mention on *Sherlock*. However, fact and fiction often bear little resemblance and what tends to get forgotten is the victims. Plans to erect a memorial to the women in Itchy Park at Christchurch, Spitalfields, have yet to materialise – only 125 years after the event.

Bibliography

Arnold, Catherine, *Underworld London* (London: Simon & Schuster UK Ltd, 2012)

Evans, Stewart P. and Rumblelow, Donald, *Jack the Ripper – Scotland Yard Investigates* (Stroud: Sutton Publishing Limited, 2006)

Chesney, Kellow, *The Victorian Underworld* (London: Penguin Books, 1991)

Flanders, Judith, *The Invention of Murder* (London: Harper Press, 2011)

Goldhill, Simon, *The Temple of Jerusalem* (London: Profile Books Ltd, 2004)

Jones, Richard, *Jack the Ripper: The Casebook* (Kent: SevenOaks, 2010)

Matthews, Rupert, *Jack the Ripper's Streets of Terror* (London: Arcturus Publishing Limited, 2013)

Moore, Pete, *The Forensics Handbook* (London: Eye Books, 2004)

Palmer, Alan, *The East End* (London: John Murray (Publishers) Ltd, 2000)

Rule, Fiona, *The Worst Street in London* (Shepperton: Ian Allan Publishing, 2008)

The Whitechapel Society, *Jack The Ripper: The Terrible Legacy* (Stroud: The History Press, 2013)

White, Jerry, *London in the 19th Century* (London: Vintage Books, 2009)

Wise, Sarah, *The Blackest Streets* (London: The Bodley Head, 2008)

Wise, Sarah, *Inconvenient People* (London: Vintage Books, 2013)

Also from The History Press

JACK THE RIPPER

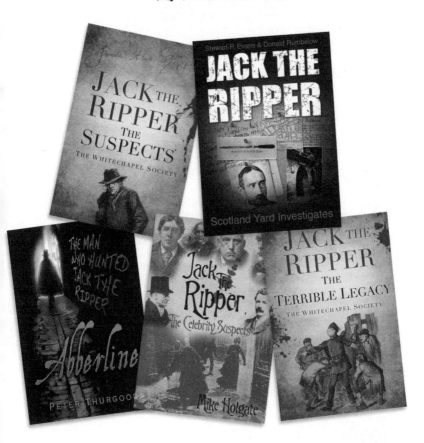